‖‖‖ ‖‖‖‖‖‖‖‖‖‖‖‖‖‖‖‖‖‖‖

W9-AJW-432

IT'S THE STORY
OF OUR LIVES . . .

The story of the first-century church and
its succeeding generations is our story.
It faced the problems of

- a tendency to take Christianity for
  granted
- loss of original urgency
- invasion of counterfeit Christianity
- retrenchment during persecution

Read **WHEN THE WAY IS NEW** to see
how the early church's problems are our
problems. And how its source of power —
God, Christ, the Holy Spirit — is also our
source of power as we of this century
face the future.

WHEN THE WAY IS NEW

CHALMER FAW

THE BRETHREN PRESS, ELGIN, ILL.

WHEN THE WAY IS NEW
Copyright © 1974 The Brethren Press

All rights reserved. Except for brief excerpts for review
purposes, no part of this book may be reproduced or used in
any form or by any means — electronic or mechanical, including
photocopying, recording or informational storage and retrieval
systems — without written permission from the publisher.

Church of the Brethren General Board, Elgin, IL 60120

Printed in the United States of America
Library of Congress Catalog Number: 74-2034
ISBN: 0-87178-929-9

CONTENTS

A WORD TO THE READER

If the church of our day is to realize something of its divine heritage and destiny it will be because the laity, along with a trained and devoted clergy, has recovered the biblical doctrine of the people of God. It is to serve as one contribution to this end, with emphasis upon the early church in the Book of Acts, that the present volume is dedicated.

Read this book as you would any other. If it interests or challenges you to study further, use the suggested readings given for each chapter. The questions for further thought may help you wrestle with some of the implications of each chapter for our day.

There is no attempt to ask easy or perfunctory questions. Quite the contrary. These are questions designed for robust thinking. Nor are there any pat or easy answers but, rather, the kind of involvement that will lead still further into contemporary church and community life.

Chalmer E. Faw

June 20, 1973
TCNN
Bukuru, Benue-Plateau State, Nigeria

1

The Community of the Resurrection

OUR AIM IN THIS BOOK is to expose ourselves to the most dynamic and vital movement ever to invade the life of man, the early Christian church. And we have the unique privilege of looking in on it from its beginnings with the resurrection of Christ.

The Christian church is a living part of each one of us whether we recognize it or not or do as much about it as we should. We lean on it, draw from it, and live in its heritage every day of our lives. Our opportunity now is to come into closer contact with that heritage and learn to understand and appreciate what is already such a vital part of us. Indeed the story of the Christian church is the story of our lives on their most significant level.

Our interest will be to gain as well-rounded an understanding of the early Christian church as is possible within the limits of this small book. We shall be interested in history and some basic historical facts. We also shall be vitally interested in our basic document, the book in the New Testament which we call The Acts of the Apostles. But we shall not be making a verse-by-verse study of Acts. That you may do on your own. What we want to do is to go back of both history and the written record to an understanding of the Christian church itself, its nature and meaning. We want to get as close as we can to the living reality of the church, find out something of the why involved in it, as well as the what and the how. We shall therefore have a great deal to say not only about history and literature, but about the theology of this dynamic reality raised up in the midst of mankind and of which we are a part. In a word, our aim will be to come to participate as fully and as consciously as possible in the significance of this divine invasion of human life.

Acts is written in a fairly simple, straightforward style, disarmingly simple for the wealth of meaning it carries. It assumes a knowledge of the mighty work of God with his people Israel — those long centuries of redemptive history of our Old Testament as well as the more recent climactic and decisive work of God in Jesus Christ. Almost casually at times, Acts will echo a mighty word out of Israel's past or refer to the earthshaking career of Christ. Or, again, it will move sketchily through whole months and years of history, highlighting only key or representative facts of the total story of the church. The reader must learn to move with the rhythm of the book, often unable to fill in the gaps. As we go along we shall get better acquainted with and come to appreciate the book's moving, readable style but our chief aim will be to participate more fully in its message in depth.

As we open our New Testaments to the first chapter of Acts and look in on the early church we note first of all that the eventful ministry and mighty resurrection of Christ are already accomplished facts. Christ has lived and taught, has died and risen again. The apostles have already been chosen and commanded through the Holy Spirit. The Risen Lord is alive and has been carrying on a forty-day ministry among his followers (matching and perhaps reflecting his forty days of preparation in the wilderness), appearing to them and instructing them in the Kingdom of God.

The burning question for the disciples now was whether or not the end of the age was to come at this time, bringing with it the long-awaited consummation of the Kingdom. Of all the limitations on the mind of man there is none more confining and baffling than the inability to see into the future. The future, even the next hour, is always veiled from our eyes. "Is this the end, the time in which the Kingdom is to be restored to Israel?" they asked the risen Lord.

"It is not for you to know the future," he explained. "That is something God controls. Your part, the part of the church, the community of the resurrection, is to receive power and be witnesses."

What seems to man like an end is so often in the sight of God but a beginning. See how this is made clear by clues here and there from the first few verses of this chapter: the commandment probably picked up from Luke 24:49 to be witnesses; the fact that they are not just disciples or learners but apostles, men with a mission and the pointing forward to the giving of the Holy Spirit and power.

"No," the risen Lord said in effect, "the Kingdom is not to be restored to Israel in the way in which you or Israel expect, but there is a Kingdom, God's Kingdom. First, God will pour forth his power, as already predicted by John the Baptist (Luke 3:16) and now about to be realized. This power will be the Holy Spirit, or God himself in his outgoing, effective reality. God himself will lay claim upon you and make you witnesses, beginning here in Jerusalem where you now are and extending outward to the ends of the earth." What a great beginning!

The Community of the Resurrection then is introduced to us as a group of very human men, God called, God commissioned and God empowered, experiencing the mighty will of the Eternal God who speaks through the living risen Lord and bestows the Holy Spirit of power. It is interesting how, though not consciously theological, these opening verses in Acts bring into action the whole trinity; God, Christ, and Holy Spirit.

Then came the ascension marking the end of the earthly ministry of Christ, the completion of his mission and the beginning of the new walk by faith on the part of the emerging church. The Lord's parting words were the words of commission; and then he was "lifted up" before them, exalted again to the right hand of God and taken out of their sight by a cloud. Not only was the future to be veiled to them, but now their risen Lord was veiled from human sight in the mystery of the invisible God.

Left without the visible support of their Lord and still awaiting the outpouring of power, the eleven (the twelve minus Judas) trudged the short distance back to the upper room in Jerusalem. Their names are listed in Acts like charter members of the new community. All of them were men who had been with Jesus. They spent the days in prayer, consultation, and (one might suppose) the searching of their scriptures (the Old Testament) seeking to understand the meaning of their existence. Their heads were awhirl with the great, strange things that had happened to them and their hearts were crying out for an answer to the problem of their identity. Who were they anyway? Why were they here? What was the meaning of all that had happened?

Not only were the eleven apostles there in the upper room but gathered about them were actually ten times that number and more, with Peter, their leader, in their midst bringing a divinely inspired suggestion to the group.

They were a broken pattern: only eleven instead of the whole number twelve, corresponding to the twelve tribes of Israel. They must correct their brokenness and in wholeness symbolize the New Israel, preparing for the messianic kingdom.

The procedure the early church fellowship followed to regain its apostolic completeness and insure the continuation of apostolic authenticity throws a great deal of light on the nature and meaning of the church. At least two aspects of this story may strike us as a bit strange. One is the seemingly artificial way in which the Apostle Peter said that "Scripture had to be fulfilled" in Judas and then, by quoting two isolated verses from Psalms 69 and 109, he used scripture to point to the solution. To choose a replacement for Judas the apostles used the old method of casting lots which, with our view of the world, smacks of chance or magic.

Peter was not proof-texting but relating the suffering and death of Jesus to those two passages from holy scripture and identifying him with Israel who is there subjected to undeserved persecution. He was also seeing the curse pronounced in these two psalms as the kind of curse which Judas, the betrayer, had brought upon himself. The matter of casting lots likewise makes more sense when we relate it to the Old Testament practice by which God's will was sought beyond mere human choice. The decision was not to be that of man, but of God through the living Lord. As Christ had chosen the original twelve so the eleven probably felt that he, rather than they, should choose the replacement for Judas. Actually, the apostles did play a part by nominating two men who met the qualifications of longtime association and witness. The lot simply decided between the two.

Much more important for our understanding of the nature and meaning of the emerging church are the less spectacular features of this whole account. We have already spoken of the Community of the Resurrection as God empowered and directed and of the apostolic nature of the community. Now let us look more closely at this church, recognizing that *this is our church* in the making.

We have been calling this church the Community of the Resurrection. It is time now to examine what we mean by this and what the resurrection of Christ signified for the church. The New Testament speaks of the resurrection as an historical reality, one which defied the honest realism of the disciples and rebuked them for their lack of faith. The risen Lord moved in their midst, not as a disembodied spirit, a phantom, but as a real person whom they recognized and from whom they received instruction, their commission, and power. True, there was mystery about the risen Lord as well there might be; he was the same Lord only gloriously free from some of the limitations of time and space. Actually there was nothing with which to compare this new reality. The demonstration of the outstretched arm of the Lord is always a mystery to the reason and mind of man. The closest analogy to it which even the most learned of theologians have discovered is God's creation of the world itself *ex nihilo,* out of nothing. So striking and earthshaking an event was bound to pose a problem for faith. To the followers of Christ, it was something too good to be true and at first they disbelieved for joy until they came to accept it gratefully, though always with awe and amazement. To the opponents of Christianity it was an idle tale or a bit of ecstatic imagination; and skeptics, sincere and misguided, have doubted it ever since. But the early Christians, after the first flush of joyful disbelief, received it as an established fact and were transformed into a divine community, the church.

Not all the meaning of the resurrection dawned upon the church right away, certainly not all in the seven-week period between Easter and Pentecost. Paul, heir of this primitive church, was later to help develop even further the central significance of it. In fact, the most profound of theologians are still wrestling with the mystery of the resurrection and its riches are still being revealed to the church. It is safe to say, however, that the reality of the resurrection in which the early church lived and worked from the very beginning was one which meant Christ's victory over all enemies, both human and spiritual. God had done a mighty work among them and the dramatic conquering of death ushered in for them a new era, the era of power and hope. The fuller realization of this era awaited, of course, the outpouring of the Spirit on Pentecost, but it was already part of their strange new world. Here the past and the future converged upon the present. Careful rereading and reinterpreting of their scriptures in the light of the tremendous fact of Christ convinced them that they were living at the end of the times in which the long promises of God were being dramatically fulfilled. At the same time they must have sensed that their biggest and best days were still ahead.

The forty days of encounter with the risen Lord and the ten days of prayer, study, and consultation between the ascension and Pentecost were more than anticipation, more than prelude. Just as we no longer speak of childhood and youth as simply prelude to adult life (implying that the latter is the only true life) but recognize in childhood and youth authentic life, so in those days of first realization of the resurrection the birth and infancy of the new community were important in their own right.

Nor is it quite accurate to call this time before Pentecost postresurrection for in the apostles' experience the resurrection was not something which ever ended, or ever could end. As a concrete historical event happening in time, the concept of "after" or "post" might be applied, but as a historical reality they were a *Community of the Resurrection,* not a postresurrection community. The resurrection was too tremendous in itself to be exhausted once it had happened. On the contrary, its full significance, at first perhaps only dimly perceived, grew and continued to grow. Furthermore, the risen Lord of the resurrection not only continued to live, but through the bestowal of power and the laying of claims upon his church, he was ever more and more alive to them as the weeks lengthened into months and years.

Therefore, though in one sense a prelude, these were days of tremendous authenticity in themselves, full to the brim with a present which was heir of a rich past and prophecy of a yet unknown but promising future. The church which was emerging was neither simply pre-Pentecostal nor postresurrection but the valid, significant church or community of the resurrection.

This authentic Community of the Resurrection was heir both of the rich heritage of the twelve tribes of Israel and of Christ's own selection and commissioning of the twelve. They were also recipients of a new commission to be witnesses everywhere. Already there were, by Christ's appointment, apostles, missionaries. The old way of reading Acts 1:8, beginning where they were in Jerusalem, then moving out to Judea and Samaria and then finally to the uttermost parts of the earth has a great deal of merit in it, though perhaps a bit too schematic for what the risen Lord had in mind. The accent in Acts seems to be upon empowering by the Holy Spirit and consequent witnessing.

The English word "witness" which translates the key word of the author of Luke 24:48 and Acts 1:8 has basically three meanings and everyone of them is appropriate to this early Christian community.

1. First, the word assumes in Greek and explicitly means in English, being witnesses *of* something, in the sense of having seen or experienced it. The apostles were witnesses of the resurrection in that they were there: they met or rather were met by the risen Lord. We use the

term "witness" in the same sense today. Something happens, let us say, an automobile accident. We set about at once to find "witnesses," people who were present when it happened and saw it: "eyewitnesses" we call them.

2. Then we speak of a witness as one who witnesses *to* something, he has seen or experienced and in this sense, to witness is to testify. This is the primary meaning of the Greek words *martus* and *martureo* as found in the New Testament. The risen Lord said of his death and resurrection, "You are witnesses of these things." That is, "You have witnessed all this and now you should go out and testify to them." This second sense of the word is also common among us today. Not only do we call for eyewitnesses of a crime or an accident, but we ask these same persons to appear in court as witnesses to others. Witnesses *of* something become witnesses *to* something as they attempt to communicate to others what they have experienced.

3. But there is a third connotation of "witness," one which springs directly out of the New Testament and will be well illustrated a bit later in the book of Acts, and that is witnessing *unto* the end, or unto the uttermost. Witnesses *of* a great event become witnesses *to* it and then if they are faithful and persistent in witness, they witness *unto* the end, regardless of whether that end be violent or natural death. We said that the Greek word for witness, a person, is *martus.* Immediately you will recognize the root of our English word for this third sense of witness, *martyr,* one who witnesses faithfully unto the uttermost, the accent being not so much on what finally happens to the person as the spirit and the faithfulness with which he witnesses. The Community of the Resurrection was given an apostolic commission spelled out in terms of witnessing.

The Community of the Resurrection, though called into being by the mighty act of God in the resurrection, was composed of some very ordinary people. We may speak of it as a divine-human venture, one initiated and empowered by God but carried out by fallible people like ourselves. The marks of human limitations have been on the men of God from earliest times. Israel's greatest leaders were not unusually talented persons, but men like Moses or Jeremiah, very hesitant in speech and self-effacing, or like Isaiah, deeply implicated in the sins of his nation. So also was it with Jesus' disciples. Take them man for man or as a group, they were not the cream of Jewish society of the first century. The four Gospels are quite frank about the slowness, hardness of heart, and, at times, downright stupidity of the disciples. In other words, they were persons like ourselves: ordinary people, possessed of all the limitations and frailties and subject to all the temptations that bedevil us. What made them the church was the act of God. Not that they were puppets. Their distinction was simply that they accepted God's gracious act and participated in it. And the fact that they were not unusually gifted or geniuses, but common people with an uncommon experience, opens the door of the church to us.

2

The Church and Fearless Witness

THE EARLY Christian church, we have said, was a divine-human adventure engaged in witnessing. Now we want to continue our quest for an understanding of that church by noting how witnessing became one of the dominant characteristics of their fellowship. Our scriptural basis will be primarily chapter 2 of Acts, with some reference to chapters 3-5.

The great new event to consider is the promised and now fulfilled outpouring of the Holy Spirit on the Day of Pentecost. As far back in Luke-Acts as the third chapter of Luke, verse 16, John the Baptist, Christ's forerunner, is quoted as saying, "I baptize you with water; but he who is mightier than I is coming . . . he will baptize you with the Holy Spirit and with fire." Nothing in the earthly career of Jesus as told by Luke quite fulfilled this promise, but it was not allowed to lapse or be forgotten. In Acts 1:4f, Jesus is quoted as reviving the promise that though John baptized with water, "Before many days you shall be baptized with the Holy Spirit." A bit later, also, he promised that they would receive power when the Holy Spirit had come upon them and would be his witnesses to the whole world, beginning in Jerusalem.

The day came on which this was to happen. It was a significant day, one of the three great festivals of the Jewish year, Pentecost or the Feast of Weeks, seven weeks or fifty days after the great feast of the Passover. ("Pentecost" is the Greek word for "fiftieth.") More significant for the imagery of Acts and for our understanding of this event for the early church is the fact that Pentecost had come to be connected in Jewish thought with the giving of the Torah or Law on Mt. Sinai. At Pentecost all Israel was invited to renew its covenant with God as it had at Mt. Sinai where the redeemed slaves from Egypt first heard the divine commandments and became a nation under God, the "people of God." Furthermore, by the first century, Pentecost had become a great international gathering of Jews from every land where they were located, swelling the city of Jerusalem from its usual size of about 50,000 people to perhaps a million. Add to this the preaching of the later prophets that Judaism should become a worldwide religion (a light to the Gentiles, in the Torah or Law the whole world should come to know the Lord), and we begin to catch a little of the tremendous scriptural and theological significance behind the simple clause: "When the day of Pentecost had come."

The Christian Pentecost is seen by some as a "new Sinai" in which God manifested himself to the assembled multitude with a mighty noise from heaven, in wind and fire, fashioning for himself a covenant people. But it went far beyond Sinai, for at Pentecost it was not Moses but the crucified and risen Lord himself who was central to the event. Here it was not the Law but God himself in the person of the Holy Spirit who came upon his chosen ones. But the discerning reader will discover to his delight that what the Torah (Law or instruction) was to Israel — the very center and meaning of all life under God — the Holy Spirit becomes in a very real sense to the Christian church. Perhaps no one was to see this more clearly than Paul who, especially in Galatians and Romans, was to show the limitations of the law and to contrast it with the glowing new life of the Spirit.

Now let us look at the simply but dramatically told story in Acts 2:1ff. Pentecost in all its wealth of meaning had arrived. The followers of Christ were "all" together in one place, words which right from the start spell universality and unity. This was the human setting. Then came the divine action: a sound from heaven (on Mt. Sinai it was thunderings and lightnings and dense smoke) like the rush of a mighty wind (in both Hebrew and Greek the word for wind or breath is also the word for Spirit) and the Spirit of God filled all the house where they were sitting. The promise had been a baptism with the Holy Spirit and fire, symbol of the divine purging and empowering. The individual flames of fire were called "tongues," no doubt pointing ahead to the gift of tongues which followed.

How are we to understand this tremendous event in terms of meaning for the early church? What about this coming of the Holy Spirit? In the Old Testament the Spirit of God was known but was never poured out on the whole people at once. It was given only to chosen individuals, and even then was temporary. In the Gospels likewise the Holy Spirit is mentioned but always in connection with Jesus, largely in the stories of his birth and baptism. One may conclude from this that before Pentecost, the Holy Spirit was not known as a reality to the disciples but only to Jesus himself. Now the Holy Spirit came upon the whole group of disciples, no longer as in the Old Testament as a temporary force but as an abiding presence.

Let us stop to think of the tremendous meaning of this for the church. The Holy Spirit is God himself going forth to work. At the creation the Spirit of God moved over the face of the waters and when God created man he breathed into him the breath (or spirit) of life. The Holy Spirit at Pentecost was God himself breathing life into the new creation, the Christian church, and preparing it to proclaim the eternal kingship of its Lord. This was to fulfill, Peter said later in his speech, the prophecy of Joel in which the Holy Spirit was to be poured out on all flesh, residing in and empowering the covenant people of God. The messianic age had come; it was not an end but a beginning, a looking forward to the complete and final victory of Christ.

The story continues: "And they were all filled with the Holy Spirit and began to speak in other tongues, as the Spirit gave them utterance." What were these other tongues and what do they mean for the church? As we compare the story told here with other parts of the New Testament we note two general possibilities so far as "tongues" are concerned. One is what seems to be the emphasis in Acts, namely that the Christians were endowed with a power to communicate in the various national languages represented: "Each one heard them speaking in his own language." But the power to speak in other languages is mentioned nowhere else in the New Testament as possessed either by these Christians or by their successors. In fact, later Paul and Barnabas at Lystra (Acts 14:11) did not seem to understand the local speech at all. Nor was such diversity of actual language necessary at Pentecost. Jews from all over the world understood each other well, if not in the Aramaic common to the East, at least in *koine* Greek spoken throughout the Roman Empire.

The sneers of the opposition at Pentecost point to the other meaning of "tongues," namely ecstatic or highly emotional speaking technically known as *glossalalia,* for the opponents mocked the apostles and called them drunk. This kind of "tongues" is what we meet with elsewhere in the New Testament. In 1 Corinthians 12 — 14 the problem is dealt with in some detail. There the speaking in tongues is clearly ecstatic speaking and Paul even says that if outsiders were to see the Christians speaking in tongues they would think them "mad" (1 Cor. 14:23).

What was Luke trying to say and what was the meaning of all this for the early church? Many suggestions have been offered to account for the blending or confusing of these two types of "tongues" in this passage. A better way to state it would be to say Luke was writing theological history, and in this instance he purposely blended theology and history, leaving a kind of double image. Luke was telling the story of how God on the Day of Pentecost invaded the life of his church so overwhelmingly that the apostles spoke as God gave them utterance, and all the world, represented by Jews from several diverse nations, heard and understood. Here was the Kingdom both in reality and in anticipation, God's gracious breakthrough in which the barriers which separate man from man, represented by human language, were transcended and man found in Christ his lost solidarity and unity. This is God's reversal of the Tower of Babel incident (Gen. 11). At Babel a man-made unity was broken and man was scattered and separated by language barriers. On Pentecost a unity from God was given as a gift from above, restoring the oneness of mankind in Christ. Men of many national backgrounds from the east, from the west, and from Africa to the south heard the gospel in their own tongues. This not only demonstrated God's transcendence of every language barrier but was also prophetic of the time when all lands, nationalities, and races will hear the gospel and enter into the Kingdom without end.

Amazement and wonder accompanied this tremendous sign and while the people were still reacting — many of them favorably but some mocking — Peter, upon whom the mantle of apostolic leadership had fallen, arose and spoke. He began with what strikes one as a very curious reply to the charge of drunkenness by citing the hour of the day. Was he implying that drunkenness is an affair of the night, whereas the apostles were of the "day"? Then he placed these tremendous happenings in their proper scriptural setting and provided a true understanding of the nature of the church.

Instead of the spirits of alcohol, said Peter, the church was filled with the Holy Spirit poured out, as Joel predicted, upon all flesh. The church lives ever in the last days, the days of the outpoured, witnessing Spirit, the prelude to even greater signs and wonders demanding decision. Then he went on to interpret this on the plane of the recent history in their midst, the mighty works of God in Jesus.

Up to this point, Peter's speech had been relatively harmless, though revolutionary, dealing with the joint witness of scripture and the Holy Spirit in their midst. Now as he interpreted the historical events of the past few years, he introduced a cutting edge that persisted throughout the remainder of the speech and was, as we shall see, a persistent part of the witness of the early church to and against society. Peter charged that, through their society, his hearers had participated in the crucifixion of Jesus. He made it quite clear that God was at work in Jesus and that men in their rebellion against Jesus were in rebellion against God himself, and that God had planned to use this rebellion to take upon himself this suffering and death. This, however, does not excuse those by whom Jesus was crucified. In fact, Peter clearly implicated everyone; all have a part in this awful deed. Nor did he lay the blame upon the Jews in distinction from anyone else. But, he said further, God raised Jesus up, untying the cords of death which had their hold on him; exalted him at the right hand of God; and poured out upon all the Holy Spirit.

The speech is a model of directness, the rapier-like thrust of the gospel into the pride and complacency of every person present. Scarcely less amazing than the daring speech itself were its tremendous results. Cut to the heart, people cried out for guidance as to what to do. Then Peter had a chance to lead them to repentance and baptism in the name of Jesus Christ for the forgiveness of sins and the promise of the gift of the Holy Spirit. Peter launched into another speech which was not recorded; we are simply told that "he testified with many other words and exhorted them." What a tremendous witness! And the results! Three thousand people were convicted and joined to the body of Christ.

The fearless witness of the early church as we have seen it thus far was initiated by God himself through the Holy Spirit. It transcended the natural barriers of all languages and national divisions and got at the heart of man's relationship to God through the crucifixion and resurrection of Christ.

This was but the beginning of witness, however. In one of his customary summary statements Luke sketched the ongoing life of the church at this time as devotion to the apostles' teaching, fellowship, the breaking of bread, and prayers. The very existence of the church acted as a dynamo of witness. The place was electric with power: "Fear came upon every soul; and many wonders and signs were done through the apostles."

Part of this group witness by the fellowship was expressed in terms of communal living in which the believers "had all things in common." This is a feature of such great interest that, rather than deal with it inadequately here, where it belongs in the context of witness, we are reserving a full scale discussion of it for the next chapter under the general heading of "The Church and Economic Problems."

Some have summarized Acts 2 — 5 in terms of the signs of the Kingdom, the same kind of signs which Jesus spoke of in his opening speech at Nazareth (Luke 4) and demonstrated throughout his career. Since these signs or proofs of the arrival of the Kingdom of Christ are also an outline of the witness of the early Christian community it would be well to look at them. The first sign is the authority to preach, well-illustrated in Peter's striking sermons and underscored again in another one of Luke's summaries (Acts 4:33): "And with great power the apostles gave their testimony to the resurrection of the Lord Jesus." The second messianic sign manifested in the early church is the forgiveness of sins, a part of Peter's call to repentance (Acts 2:38). The third is the healing of the sick, illustrated by the cure of the lame man in the temple in Chapter 3. The fourth and climaxing messianic sign is the proclamation of victory over the kingdoms of this world, as demonstrated in the deeds of the apostles in Acts 4 and 5.

In witnessing, then, the church was simply continuing the works that Jesus himself began, and the power by which it witnessed was clearly given by God himself in the Holy Spirit. The fearlessness by which the apostles spoke arose not because they were made of more courageous stuff than other men, for they were as we have said before, quite ordinary folk. Their fearlessness arose from being controlled by the Holy Spirit who gave them utterance. They never stopped to think about how they were doing or what others would say. They simply did what God inspired them as a group to do with the faith and abandon which can come only to those who are completely dedicated to Christ and faithfully attempting to follow him.

Let us note how this worked out. First Peter and John healed a lame man "in the name of Jesus Christ of Nazareth" and amazed the populace. This drew a crowd and Peter addressed the people, explaining that the healing was by the power of Jesus whom they had delivered to be killed. Again he gave the call to repentance for the forgiveness of sins. The presence of a large crowd attracted the temple authorities who put Peter and John in custody. The next day Peter gave the same fearless witness to the high court, the Sanhedrin itself, charging again that he whom they had put to death had been raised by God in power and by this power the cripple had been healed. The court was amazed at their boldness but could not gainsay the mighty deed for the evidence stood there before them. Then quite lamely the authorities attempted to prevent Peter and John from witnessing, but the apostles were determined to listen to God rather than to them. They returned to their Christian group and all lifted their voices in prayer. Instead of asking that the opposition be softened, however, they asked that God would help them speak the word with boldness. The prayer was answered as the place was shaken and they were again filled with the Holy Spirit and spoke with new daring. After a similar encounter (recorded in chapter 5), they went their way "rejoicing that they were counted worthy to suffer dishonor for the name." This was the kind of intrepid witness the spirit-filled church demonstrated.

God by his Holy Spirit was launching his offensive against all evil within man and society. God's church carried on this offensive in the fearlessness of men totally committed to Christ. But evil and the evil powers counterattacked, and the result was persecution and attempted intimidation. The church, however, responded with faithfulness and persistent witness far beyond its own human strength. Its witness was born of complete trust in the God who raised the crucified Jesus from the dead.

One statement that Peter made in his first recorded appearance before the Sanhedrin so sharply puts the issue that Christians ever since have been tempted to tone it down. Speaking of Jesus Christ he said, "There is salvation in no one else, for there is no other name under heaven given among men by which we must be saved." Not only was the church counterattacking evil by the power of the risen Lord, it was claiming that Christ is ultimate. While at first this may appear arrogant or intolerant, it is but the logical consequence of a resurrection that is unique and a power of God that is supreme. Relativism here would be a weakening of the central claim of Christianity that God meets man decisively and supremely in Jesus Christ. The early church was sure at this point. The new age of the righteous rule of God in Christ had begun and it stands in sharp judgment upon the old era of human perversity and brokenness.

For the early church witness meant living, acting, and speaking faithfully within the new age of the gospel of Jesus Christ, God's unique Word, so that the new era of Christ would impinge upon and finally replace the old by God's action.

3

The Church and Economic Problems

SO FAR WE HAVE discovered that the early church was the
community of believers created by the resurrection, engaging in fearless witness of and to their faith. Now we
want to consider a phase of life in the early Christian community that is mentioned quite frequently in our source-
book, Acts. Discussion of the church and the economic
life of its people should throw considerable light on the
nature of the church itself.

First let us observe that Luke-Acts, of which our text-
book Acts is the second volume, more than any other
writing in the New Testament is interested in economic
problems. In the Gospel of Luke a surprising number of
parables and other teachings of Jesus found only in that
book revolve around matters of property and finance, for
example, the rich man and Lazarus, the poor widow and
the obdurate judge, the unrighteous steward. Even the
much-loved story of the prodigal son, found only in Luke,

is not without its economic side with its interest in dividing and squandering the father's property, famine in the land, destitution of the son, and even slaying the fatted calf after the return. Likewise throughout Acts there is a genuine interest shown in the impact Christianity has upon the financial or economic aspects of life.

Let us look closely at three situations from the first six chapters of Acts in which economic problems entered the picture and seek to gain from them some understanding of this issue as a whole.

In chapter two, we worked around the intriguing reference to the community of goods practiced by the Jerusalem church. Luke referred to this twice in his summaries (Acts 2:43-47 and 4:32-37). The story of Ananias and Sapphira (Acts 5:1-11) likewise presupposes this situation. In the context of Holy Spirit power and witness, of signs and wonders done through the apostles, of the arrival of the new era and the expectation of greater things to come, the Jerusalem believers "had all things in common, sold their possessions and goods and distributed them to all, as any had need." As a result of their having everything in common "there was not a needy person among them."

The first and basic thing to note is that this was not a planned economic arrangement but one springing spontaneously from the outpouring of the Holy Spirit. The believers were like a colony of God-inspired people newly landed in a strange and unfriendly world. They lived together, worshiped together, ate together, and shared freely with one another on every level. Not that they were withdrawn from society — quite the contrary: they stayed on in the midst of a bustling city, participated in the daily worship in the temple, mingled with the populace and, when occasion arose, gave their testimony as we have seen. What they did was motivated by the belief that the new age had come and that they, as members of the new age, should live in fellowship and sharing until their Lord returned to consummate the Kingdom. Nothing is said here specifically about the expectation of the early return of the Lord as undergirding their communal life. The reason may be that Luke was writing from the later historical perspective of the ongoing church. But what we know otherwise of the earliest hopes and views of the church would lead us to see that the eschatological hope (the expectation of an imminent return of Christ) played an important part in this situation.

We wish we knew more about the actual life of these early Christians. Luke's references are general summaries only and leave us with the necessity of using our imaginations. Their worship consisted of daily attendance at the temple "together." But was "breaking bread in their homes" also an act of worship? Opinions differ — all the way from regarding this as the celebration of Holy Communion itself to taking it as simply communal meals with only incidental religious significance. Certainly we can say that they were a worshiping community whose whole life had religious significance. Their breaking bread together (an expression used of the eucharist, but also a familiar Jewish expression for the beginning of any meal) is a vital part of their eschatological Community of the Resurrection. Therefore it is with religious meaning that Luke said, "They partook of food with glad and generous hearts, praising God and having favor with all the people." In other words, if their breaking of bread together was not a form of Holy Communion, it at least had religious and perhaps sacramental significance.

New light has been thrown on this practice of communal living by the Dead Sea Scrolls and the remains of the community at Qumran along the Dead Sea where the scrolls were produced. This community which was still being occupied at the time of our story in Acts had a large banquet hall with an adequate pantry room adjacent.

In this hall the fully initiated members of the community ate their meals in great sanctity in anticipation of the messianic banquet of the age to come.

We cannot be sure of any direct line of connection between the Essenes of Qumran and the early Christian church in Jerusalem, but there are enough similarities between the two groups on this matter of communal living and community of goods for us to learn from them. Both communities were deeply devoted to a present and a coming Kingdom of God. Both regarded themselves as persons of the New Covenant (New Testament). The members of both groups shared their resources with one another and partook of communal meals which had messianic significance.

To keep the record straight, however, we must note some important differences. In the writings of Qumran there are only veiled and uncertain references to a messiah, or in some documents two anointed ones, a priestly and a lay messiah. The whole Jerusalem church, on the other hand, was based on the firm conviction that Messiah had come in the person of Jesus of Nazareth who had lived, died, and been raised from the dead in their midst. The Qumran society was withdrawn from the world in its wilderness dwelling and maintained a stricter order of discipline, representing the ultimate in legalistic rigor. The Jerusalem Christians, on the other hand, lived and worked in the teeming city of Jerusalem and, so far as we know, were governed not by stern legalistic rules of the order but by a free and exuberant Spirit. The community of goods at Qumran was compulsory and an integral part of the planned economy of the society. The evidence of Acts points to the fact that among the early Christians the selling of property and turning it over to the group, while highly approved, was entirely voluntary. Joseph Barnabas, for example, was praised for his generosity because he sold a field which belonged to him and brought the money to the apostles; and Ananias was told that while his land remained unsold it was his own and even after it was sold the proceeds were at his disposal. Members of the church continued to own private property, as for example, Mary the mother of Mark (Acts 12:12).

The community of goods among these Christians was a result of their deep devotion, and not an end in itself or a rule of the order. Just as they shared the spiritual blessings of God, so they also shared the material. God opened their hearts and opened their pocketbooks as well. Since everything belonged to God the Creator and his Son Jesus Christ and they were but stewards of the divine wealth, it was with deepest theological awareness that "no one said that any of the things which he possessed was his own."

Lest we confuse the practice of the Jerusalem church with certain modern forms of communal living, let us note also that theirs was a communism not of production but of distribution and consumption. Nothing is said about their producing material wealth in common, so little was this a planned economy.

How long this voluntary sharing lasted, we have no way of knowing. There is no evidence that it was reproduced in any of the other Christian fellowships, although something of the close fellowship and eating together is in evidence later at Antioch (Gal. 2:12), and in a somewhat corrupted form at Corinth (1 Cor. 11:20-22). Perhaps we may assume that after a few years the practice gradually became cumbersome and died out. There is a possibility that the later poverty of the Jerusalem church which prompted repeated sending of relief goods was due not only to the recurrent famines of the land but also to the fact that the tangible assets of the Christian community had been consumed through the years without adequate replacement (Acts 1:27-30; 24:17; 1 Cor. 16:1-4; 2 Cor. 8, 9; Rom. 15:25f).

One of the strangest stories of the whole book of Acts is the tragic fate which met Ananias and his wife Sapphira. In some respects it sounds like something out of the darker pages of the Old Testament, like the sin of Achar or the rebellion of Korah. Some commentators agree that the story is "frankly repulsive." But to pass such judgment is to miss the whole point of the story.

First we must realize that this account is to be taken in contrast with one which precedes it praising Barnabas for his wholehearted generosity. Together the two stories form a pair, emphasizing respectively good discipleship and its blessings and hypocritical discipleship and its curse. To omit either one of these aspects would be to make an incomplete report. So it was throughout the whole teaching, preaching, and ministry of Jesus. There were those who received his blessing, but also others who drew from him woes and pronouncements of destruction.

As far as the economics of the early church are concerned, this story shows us that the selling of property was not compulsory. The sin of this self-seeking couple was not that they failed to turn over their property to the church, or even that they withheld part of the proceeds for themselves. Their sin was that they lied to the Holy Spirit. Under the social pressure or the desire for status they sold a piece of property and went through the motions of contributing the total proceeds to the church. But they withheld some of it and lied both to God and the apostles about it. Their sin was deliberate deception.

But why did the punishment have to be so severe? Some commentators see in this story a drastic example of early Christian discipline. The part played by the Apostle Peter as the chief disciplinarian is sometimes stressed. But this is not to read the story as Luke portrayed it. Peter was the spokesman for God's Spirit. Death was the punishment for both Ananias and his wife meted out by God himself, not by the church, nor by Peter. A sentimental or unrealistic doctrine of God would not permit the One who created life the right to terminate it. "The Lord giveth and the Lord taketh away, blessed be the name of the Lord" is a statement which not only fits the story of Job, but accords also with the sovereign character of God as we find it both in the teachings of Jesus and the writings of the remainder of the New Testament.

This story tells us that the early church was engaged in no mere child's play, but in a matter of life and death — the Kingdom of God leading to life and its opposite, the Kingdom of Evil leading to death. We have spoken before of the tremendous power of Holy Spirit possession. An almost electric-like power to perform signs and wonders had been generated in the community. We could call it high-voltage Christianity with great potential for life or death. In Ananias and Sapphira we find a couple who ran afoul of this power and whose sin became a dramatic example to believer and unbeliever alike. Little wonder that Luke added to the story: "And great fear came upon the whole church, and upon all who heard of these things." Here good and evil and their consequences stand clearly revealed. Let there be no dabbling in hypocrisy or duplicity from this time on.

The third incident with which we are concerned in this inquiry in the church and economic issues is recorded in the first few verses of chapter six of Acts. In all likelihood, considerable time had passed unmarked by the author. The church had grown not only in numbers but in cultural complexity. The immediate problem was one which arose between the Greek or Hellenistic element in the church and the Hebraic stock. Whatever the precise meaning of these distinctions, here is evidence of a tension that had economic repercussions. The Hellenists complained that their widows were being neglected in the daily distribution. We wish we knew more about what was happening. Apparently the earliest spontaneous acts of benevolence had been replaced by some kind of systematic distribution to those in need, widows and other dependents. Apparently, also, a revision in organization was already overdue. The twelve were not willing to give up preaching to take on more administrative work. It has been suggested in the light of the association of "tables" with accounting in first-century papyri, that the twelve were saying that it was not right that they should give up preaching to spend their time in financial administration. Though there are several obscure aspects of the story, the direction is clear. Instead of burdening the twelve apostles with concern for the distribution of funds or supplies, seven new men were chosen to take charge of the work. Since those chosen all bore Greek names and one was a former Gentile, a proselyte to Judaism, it is possible to read verse 3 as addressed primarily to the Hellenists themselves, "Pick out from among you [Hellenists] seven men of good repute and full of the Spirit and wisdom."

While these men were chosen in response to an economic need, their work more nearly corresponded to that of the apostles themselves. Certainly what we know of the activities of Stephen, the invincible witness to Christ in the Hellenistic synagogues and the first Christian martyr, and of Philip, the missionary to Samaria, reminds us of the work of the twelve. It has been suggested, and not without considerable plausibility, that the seven (even the number is significant) became the apostles for the Hellenistic or Greek-minded wing of the church, paralleling somewhat the functions of the twelve apostles over the Hebraic church. What happened to the daily distribution or the widows of the Hellenists who were being neglected we are not told, but we assume that the problem was met and human needs were cared for by this new arrangement.

The question that must certainly be lurking in our minds is: what light do these accounts in Acts throw on the church and economic problems of our day? Without attempting anything like a complete answer to this question we could perhaps make a few observations. First, economic needs and concerns were regarded by the early church as important. They were not overlooked or by-passed. It needs to be said, however, that economic problems were not approached as a present-day economist might approach them, but rather as an aspect of Christian brotherhood. Second, economic problems were considered important but not the most important problems. They were subordinated, it is fair to say, to the total Christian witness. The third thing that needs to be said is that the economic problems which the church dealt with were the problems of their own group. They made no attempt to straighten out or tamper with the economic system of all Jerusalem, much less that of the Roman Empire. This does not mean that the church today (comprising, as it does, such a higher percentage of the total population and operating within a democratic system where individuals are made more responsible for society) should not take a hand in influencing the economic systems of our day. It simply says that it would be erroneous to use the early Christians as an example of any type of direct economic action outside their own Christian community.

The spirit of the economic interest of the early church is its most significant contribution to all time. Beginning with God's creational ownership of all the earth, they did not regard their possessions as belonging to themselves but to God, and so shared them freely with their brothers. They took care of everyone in need. The Spirit was at work among them and a couple who dared conspire against the Spirit suffered dire consequences. Then when earlier administrative procedures were insufficient to care for the economic needs of a growing membership, the church took steps, in the spirit of prayer and devotion, to bring the organization up to date with the need.

4

The Church Breaks With Provincialism

VERY FEW ECONOMIC problems are solely economic in origin and certainly the problem posed by the Hellenists in the church is no exception. Back of the neglect of the Hellenistic widows in the first place and perhaps back of the murmuring by the Hellenist Christians against the Hebrew Christians were some personal and ideological differences which led to the discrimination. It is only human that this be so. Let us look at it a little more closely.

Who were the "Hellenists" and the "Hebrews" of Acts 6:1? Several theories have been advanced and we cannot be absolutely certain of any one answer. One explanation is that there was primarily a difference in religious point of view: the "Hebrews" were the strict Jews of the Pharisee type and the Hellenists, although also Jews, were less orthodox. The difficulty is that this explanation would tend to class Peter and the twelve as Jewish Christians of the strict Pharisaic type. Besides, Luke often used other terminology in referring to conservative Judaistic Christians, calling them either the circumcision party (Acts 11:2 and elsewhere) or, in one instance, disciples of the party of the Pharisees (Acts 15:5). A more satisfactory explanation is that while both groups were Jews, the difference was primarily cultural and linguistic. The "Hebrews" were those whose native tongue was Semitic (Hebrew or Aramaic) although they may also have spoken Greek; while the Hellenists were those whose mother tongue and perhaps only language was Greek. This would mean that the "Hebrew" Christians were primarily Semitic in orientation, culture, and language and the "Hellenist" Christians primarily Greek in approach. The "Hebrews" might be either Palestinian or foreign born; most all the "Hellenists" would be foreign-born Jews reared in centers of Graeco-Roman culture. Paul, for example, by calling himself a "Hebrew born of Hebrews" (Phil. 3:5) meant that his first language was Semitic, but we know he also spoke Greek. In point of view, however, while brought up a strict Pharisee, as a Christian he was anything but a conservative; in fact he was the ringleader of the liberal, pro-Gentile party.

In the Jerusalem church the Greek-speaking Hellenists, often unable to understand the Hebraic language and thought forms must have felt at times that they were "not wanted" in the larger fellowship or that someone was discriminating against them. At the same time, as members of the body of Christ, they must have realized that in Christ all differences can be transcended.

What did the Jerusalem church do about these language and cultural differences? Did they let them divide the church or cause continual strife? Or did they permit one group to go on as a neglected and underprivileged minority? We know they did not. They asked this new group to choose some of their ablest and most spiritual men and gave them the official blessing of the whole church, the laying on of hands. These men became not only the overseers of the new cultural group but apparently also their spokesmen and witnesses to the world.

The story of Stephen is an exciting one. Nothing whatever is said of his economic administration or his deacon duties, but as a witness for the gospel he was invincible. No one could "withstand the wisdom and the Spirit with which he spoke." The only way the opposition could stop him was a method resorted to even today when the truth gets too close and too hot; they stirred up the people against him, started a smear campaign, had him up before their court, and framed him. The whole story is a replay of the trial and crucifixion of Jesus. They bribed false witnesses, but God was with him all the way; "his face was like the face of an angel."

Unlike Jesus, however, Stephen let them have it straight. Though God had been more than kind and solicitous with the Hebrew nation, Stephen said, calling them and leading them out of one trouble after another, the Hebrew people had always been a stiff-necked and rebellious lot. They murmured against Moses, put Aaron to making them a golden calf, and thought they could enclose God in a house. God, the great God of the universe, he said, "does not dwell in houses made with hands." And then by accusing the leaders of the people of always resisting the Holy Spirit, persecuting the prophets, and betraying and murdering their own Messiah, Stephen sealed his death warrant. Too enraged even to take a vote, the council rushed on him as one man, casting him out of the city and stoning him. What a man! What a witness!

You may be saying, "What a fool!" This was no way to win friends and influence people. Perhaps not, but the forthright witness of this minority group leader, this Hellenist preacher of an unfettered, unprovincial God made an impact that day, not only upon his own followers and all Christendom until now, but upon a contemporary man of even greater potential than he, one destined some day to become Christianity's greatest force in breaking with provincialism, Saul of Tarsus.

What the Hebrew Christians thought of this Hellenistic firebrand whom they had ordained by the laying on of hands we have no way of knowing. Quite likely he was a controversial figure inside the church as well as outside it. Absolutists are never fully appreciated by more cautious people, even though they may speak for the conscience of those same people. Stephen went down under a pile of stones, but those stones erected a monument to this first Christian martyr, this witness-unto-the-uttermost, which has outlived the memory of all who slew him, save one. A firebrand himself, Saul from that day forth began to enter the thrilling drama, first as antagonist and then as protagonist of the gospel which breaks all bonds.

The witness of Stephen touched off a great persecution against the church which drove the Christians out of their sectarian center in Jerusalem. At this point another one of the Hellenist leaders entered the story, Philip, whose name was as Greek as Alexander the Great, son of the first great Philip. Philip the evangelist (not to be confused with the apostle by that name), like Stephen, was filled with the Holy Spirit and performed signs and wonders. And what did he do? Driven out from the Holy City because he had the Holy Spirit he went down to Samaria. Every direction from Jerusalem is "down," not only from the standpoint of altitude, but theologically down. This way of thinking and speaking was good, in a way, for it emphasized the transcendent glory of God who made his home in Jerusalem. But it was bad, very bad, as the expression of any who fancied that God was confined to Jerusalem or who felt that because they lived or worshiped in Jerusalem, every direction away from them was down.

Of all the people whom the Jews most roundly hated, the most despised were the Samaritans. Not outright Gentiles or pagans, they were worse. They were in the eyes of the Jews the degenerate and mongrelized descendants of the former Northern Kingdom of Israel, the kingdom which centuries before its collapse set up bull worship at Bethel under Jeroboam the First.

Two centuries of rivalry and warfare between North and South followed and then Samaria was captured by the Assyrians and most of its leaders were carried into captivity and scattered among the nations, the so-called Ten Lost Tribes. In their place the Assyrians brought in pagans of all sorts and planted them in the land. Rivalry turned to bitterness many years later when the Southern Kingdom attempted to reestablish itself in Jerusalem under Nehemiah and Ezra. The Samaritans, already strong in their own rebuilt city, opposed the refortifying of Jerusalem and resented the strict marriage laws prompted by Ezra. There were recriminations and counterrecriminations and in the course of time the Samaritans built their own temple on Mt. Gerizim.

In 128 BC a Jewish ruler, John Hyrcanus, a successor of the great Judas Maccabee, marched into Samaria in force and destroyed the Samaritan temple. Thus bitterness and hostility smouldered on over many centuries, contributing to the situation prevailing at the time of Jesus, and made immortal in the brilliant understatement that "Jews have no dealings with Samaritans" (John 4:19). One would note that precisely because there were so many ties of nationality, religion, and geography between the two groups, the hatreds which did arise rankled the more deeply, as bad blood among relatives always has a way of doing.

The revolutionary story of the Good Samaritan, also

a Lukan exclusive, turns upon the transcending of this deep hatred. This is true also of the story of Jesus and the Samaritan woman, with Jesus' word about "the fields white unto the harvest" (which, by the way, were Samaritan fields) and the account of the Christianizing of the Samaritan village of Sychar later in the same narrative (John 4).

Philip went down to a city of Samaria. Its name, if known, is not revealed. The point is the tremendous success he had there and his encounter with a religious leader named Simon, known to us in other early Christian sources as Simon Magus, or Simon the Sorcerer. Philip's witness was so powerful that he first won over a large number of Simon's followers and then Simon himself. So the Community of the Resurrection, begun in Jerusalem, the Holy City of the Jews, spread to the land of the hated Samaritans. There is no indication that the Samaritans became second-class Christians, unless it is the move which the Jerusalem church took of sending Peter and John to Samaria to investigate and to bestow the Holy Spirit. The assumption was that the Holy Spirit is given only at apostolic action and yet there were baffling exceptions. When the free Spirit of God is at work, there is no predictable consistency of form or order, much as we logically-minded persons would like to see it. Might it not be that our confusion at the freedom of the Spirit which "blows where it wills" is akin to the misguided attempt of Simon Magus to purchase and so control the Holy Spirit for his own ends? We too would like to control the movement of the Spirit through proper rites and procedures, turning it on or off to suit our wills, contrary to the implication of the whole New Testament that all this is a gift of God and not to be contained or controlled in any scheme of man's doing.

The provincially-minded Christian church beginning first among predominately Semitic peoples had begun to overcome its provincialism by recognizing the claims and character of the Hellenists, or Greek-cultured Jewish Christians. Now they advanced a step further by seeing the Holy Spirit work among the despised Samaritans with their mixed blood and strange, conservative religion.

The foot-loose Philip got himself into yet another intercultural and even interracial situation with strange disregard for the strict lines laid down by the purists and proper people. His pioneer work done in opening Samaria to the continued working of the apostles who preached "the gospel to many villages of the Samaritans," Philip was commanded by an angel of the Lord to go south to the road from Jerusalem to Gaza.

On the road to Gaza Philip met an Ethiopian. Nothing is said about the man's color. The New Testament is peculiarly color-blind when it comes to people. The pigment of skin meant no more than the color of eyes or shape of nose, all purely external. This man was an African from the ancient country of Ethiopia, high in government service, the chief treasurer to the queen. He was a religiously minded man, either a Jew or inquirer into Judaism, for he had gone to Jerusalem to worship and possessed a copy of the Scriptures. Again without consulting the authorities in Jerusalem, but commanded by the authority of the Spirit of Almighty God, Philip approached the man and interpreted to him the passage from Isaiah 53 as referring to Christ. Before long the Ethiopian was asking for Christian baptism and received it; and then before any one could stop him, Philip was on his way back up around Azotus and the Ethiopian treasurer was "on his way rejoicing" to the court of Queen Candace.

Nothing more is told about this encounter nor its aftermath. Nor is any mention made of an investigation by the Jerusalem apostles. The writer was interested primarily in the witness of the church to another part of the world, for the church proclaims a gospel for all nations.

Here then is the record: The Christian church, born within the fold of Judaism and cradled in the capital city of Jerusalem, had begun to break the bonds of provincialism. Nor was this the end; there was much more to come. But consider these types of outgrown provincialism:

1. *The provincialism of language.* Hebrew was the language of the sacred scriptures and of Judaism. It and its cousin Semitic language, Aramaic, were the basic languages also of the New Israel, the Christian church. Christ himself and all the twelve apostles were, so far as we know, at home in these Semitic languages. Though occasional contacts with Greek-speaking people are mentioned in the four Gospels, the gospel proclamation and teaching were pretty much a Semitic language affair, with all the important concepts wedded to Hebraic ways of thinking. There came to be a considerable number of Christians who were not at home in any Semitic language. So far as the typical Hebrew Christian was concerned, these Hellenists, though basically good-hearted and possessing all the marks of authentic Christianity, were rather strange at one point. They could not understand the language and the teachings of Jesus without translation. And as for speaking, what these Hellenists would say in expression of their Christian faith, would be, in the thinking of provincial Hebrew Christians, "all Greek to me."

2. Or, consider *the provincialism of national and religious prejudice.* If you are brought up from childhood to hate and despise a certain race or nation of people and this is in the very fabric of your everyday speech, then provincialism has gone very deep. You can, for example, quite innocently call somebody "an Indian giver," unconscious of the injustice you do the Indian American. If you are so conditioned toward any group of people that contempt has become a part of every thought and word, then there is quite a bit of provincialism to be rooted out and melted away and overcome before you can treat that

45

group as first-class human beings, much less as full brothers in Jesus Christ. "Samaritan" was a nasty name among the Jews. One time the opponents of Jesus, unable to cope with him otherwise and wishing to pin a dirty label on him, said, "Are we not right in saying that you are a Samaritan and have a demon?" (John 8:48).

3. *The provincialism of race and color.* If Philip had a personal feeling about Africans, he never mentioned it. If Luke considered an Ethiopian as a different sort of creature, he made no point of it. Yes, there are particularities of race, nationality, complexion, even color, but they are like the thousands of other ways in which we differ. On the one hand they may be inconsequential and no more worth thinking about than say, refusing to sit by a person on the plane because he has a pug nose.

On the other hand, real differences may be regarded as diverse gifts to be brought in to enrich the fellowship which we have in Christ.

There is little said in Acts about the theological significance of the church's gradual triumph over its inherent provincialisms. Luke was more concerned simply to tell the story and let it speak for itself. Not until we come to the really big provincial boundary between Judaism and paganism shall we note anything of the real struggle like that of Peter as he met Cornelius. But already in actual practice the early church, led by the Spirit of the Creator of heaven and earth and of all mankind and filled with the gospel of the One who died for all men, was getting involved in provincialism-cracking experiences. Reflections on this must have occurred but are not mentioned. Already the church was beginning to experience the affirmation of the body of Christ across all human differences: finding in some aspects only the trivial and incidental things to overlook and in others the divine variety that is not only the spice but the vital enrichment of life.

5

The Church and the Gentile Challenge

IN A SENSE THIS chapter on the early church and the Gentile challenge is a continuation of the problem of provincialism, only more intense and epoch-making. After all, the Hellenists, among whom Christianity began to spread, were Jews. The Samaritans were people of the Torah who possessed much in common with the Judean Jews. Even the Ethiopian was likely either a Jew or a proselyte. But the big new boundary to cross in the journey out of provincialism was the gulf which separated Jew from Gentile.

Things soon began to happen. The old wineskins of exclusiveness could no longer contain the new wine of the gospel and as they burst they overflowed to a people outside the covenant of Israel who were thirsty for the good news.

This crossing of the divide between Jewish and related groups on the one hand and the vast pagan world on the other is told in great detail and with no little drama and humor in the story of Cornelius (Acts 10, 11). There may have been other Gentiles won to the church in less dramatic ways, as reflected in the work of the unnamed missionaries who founded the church at Antioch. But Cornelius' conversion gives us an opportunity to look at the problem at close range and understand something of both the obstacles and the mighty push of the Spirit of Christ. What were the Christians to do about the great mass of people of the Roman Empire for whom Christ died but who did not enjoy the advantages of Judaism?

The apostles were from the start chosen to be missionaries to carry the gospel to the ends of the world. Thus far they had been tied up in affairs in Jerusalem and had not gone out. In fact, the only Christians to leave Jerusalem in any numbers were those driven out by persecution, Hellenists like Philip and others left unnamed. But the sacrificial death and resurrection of the Lord, the commissioning of the Apostles, the worldwide symbolism of Pentecost, the crossing of boundaries into Samaria, and the conversion of an Ethiopian have all pointed in the direction of worldwide outreach.

Peter, the leader of the church, was touring the country. We have seen how he and John had been sent into Samaria to confirm the converts made there by Philip. Apparently Christian groups had begun to spring up here and there all around Judea, and Peter was moving about among them. We find him first at Lydda where he healed a paralyzed man. And then at Joppa there was another Christian group and one of its number, Tabitha, or Dorcas as we know her, had died and Peter was sent for. A remarkable miracle was worked through him and she was raised from the dead. This created such a stir that Peter stayed on at Joppa awhile and helped reap the harvest, but still among Jewish people.

At Joppa, Peter lived with a certain Simon the tanner. Since the tanning of hides with its contact with dead bodies and its overwhelming smells was, in the opinion of the strict Jew, one of the unclean occupations, Peter was already showing signs of broadened sympathies. Even so he was hardly prepared for what was to happen.

The break-through began with a Roman army officer. He was a devout man, a "God-fearer," a term which Luke customarily used of Gentiles who were inquirers in Judaism and ripe for the gospel. The action was directed by God himself by his Spirit. In this new step forward the Spirit led the church through Simon Peter. Peter did not think up the idea on his own. It is true of most of us that unless nudged or forced to challenge our prejudices by something outside ourselves we do not usually do so. So near and so dear to us are most of our provincialisms that we do not give them up without being forced to. In fact, we are often not even aware of them without outside help.

Working simultaneously at both ends of the line in the context of prayer, the Spirit of God succeeded in bringing these two diverse men together, Peter the Hebrew Christian and Cornelius the devout Gentile. At Caesarea Cornelius had a vision to which he reacted in terror and reverent obedience. At Joppa Peter fell asleep during a lunchtime prayer vigil. His vision was a curious one. On a sheet let down from heaven (the source and direction here are important) were all kinds of animals, reptiles, and birds. In telling about this vision later (Acts 11:6) Peter mentioned "beasts of prey," probably indicating that it was a motley array of unclean, carnivorous animals: hyenas, vultures, pythons, maybe a pig or two, and other repulsive creatures. Though commanded by the Lord to "Rise, kill and eat," Peter in his dream could not bring himself to do so. "No, Lord," he found himself saying in his sleep, "I have never eaten anything that is common or unclean." Although somewhat careless in his habits (from the viewpoint of the strict Pharisee) Peter nevertheless had been a good Jew all his life and had kept the lines of distinction between Jew and Gentile sharply defined. But the Spirit was insistent, "What God has cleansed, you must not call common." "What? All kinds of unclean animals cleansed by God? Preposterous!" his subconscious mind screamed out. But this happened three times over, like every true sign from heaven, and he was convinced that he really was dreaming it, and not just dreaming that he dreamed it.

We must pause here and consider the fact that the Jewish taboos against certain foods and their very careful laws against mixing with the pagans about them arose for very good reasons: to keep the people of God pure in body, mind, and spirit. It is doubtful if the Jewish religion or culture would ever have survived had they not built around their people fences of prohibition and taboo which were not to be taken lightly. Throughout most of Israelite history, the pagans round about and often in the midst of the chosen people were of such idolatrous character and such degraded morals that to mix or intermarry indiscriminately with them would have meant religious and national suicide. The trouble was that the virtue of maintaining a people holy unto the Lord so easily got twisted and tortured into prideful separation and the easy assumption that it was by one's own good works that he maintained his position in the household of God or that one's virtue had achieved this. Deep within Judaism were springs of genuine humility which could have meant bringing all of life completely and constantly under the judgment of God, letting him decide among the peoples. But centuries of strife, suffering, and general hardening of the religious arteries had brought about the condition now illustrated in Simon Peter with whom the Spirit must contend.

So forthright was Cornelius' obedience to the vision which he had received that by the time Peter had finished his sleep and was still wondering about the strange experience, the Roman officer's men were outside awaiting him. The Spirit prompted Peter to invite the men in, Gentiles though they were, to share with him his overdue dinner and stay with him overnight. Already he was getting involved. But in his mind kept ringing the words of the vision, "What God has cleansed, you must not call common or unclean."

The next day the group started out. Peter, sensing the beginning of something big and maybe dangerous, took along six good Jewish Christians to give him support and be witnesses of the encounter with the Gentiles. After two days they were in Caesarea, the seat of the provincial government of Palestine where the procurators and their military retinues lived. Cornelius had been waiting for their return and welcomed them with a house full of friends and relatives.

Peter had misgivings as he stepped across the threshold into a Gentile home, violating the taboos in which he had been steeped from childhood. Cornelius was even more visibly moved and prostrated himself before Peter as before a god. Shocked by the idolatry of such an act, Peter lifted him to his feet with the words, "Stand up; I too am just a man." Inside the house, Peter blurted out right away his deep-seated feelings against associating with or visiting a Gentile, "one of another nation" as he put it. But he recognized that God had shown him that he was not to call any man common or unclean. Already he had made an application of the dream.

Now we are on the inside of the situation: the deep-seated prejudices of Peter, the gradual loosening up of his prejudices through divine revelation, and his own action, leading from one step of revelation and obedience to another.

After a statement by Cornelius bringing Peter up to date on his side of the story, Peter spoke the gospel message. His opening statement is noteworthy: that God shows no partiality but receives anyone of any nation who fears him (basic faith) and does what is right (response in obedience). There is a play here on words not immediately apparent in the English. The Greek word for "nation" in the plural is the word for "Gentiles" and to say that God accepts men of all nations means he includes the Gentiles in the divine grace.

While Peter was proclaiming the gospel message, the Holy Spirit fell on all who heard the word, reenacting Petecost for the Gentiles. Although he was sure that he had been led by the Spirit of God, seeing the Holy Spirit descend upon Cornelius and his entire household convinced Peter beyond all doubt. He was quick to order baptism for these who, as he put it, "have received the Holy Spirit just as we have." God himself had chosen the Gentiles for his church and no one, least of all the apostle Peter, would oppose him.

The sequel to the story of Cornelius is equally revealing on the matter of breaking across the Jew-Gentile barrier. It may be all right for one man to cross over, under the impulse of a dramatic experience, but the elders back in Jerusalem (especially those of the more conservative group, now called for the first time the "circumcision party") had not had such an experience. For them the barriers still existed as a divine command. "Why did you go to uncircumcised men and eat with them?" they challenged Peter.

Peter's reply to his Jerusalem critics was a recital of the whole story as seen from his standpoint. He added clarification giving the direct line of promise and fulfillment from John the Baptist's prediction of Holy Spirit baptism through the great experience of Pentecost to the outpouring of the Spirit on the Gentiles. Here was powerful proof that the mission to the Gentiles was divinely inspired and directed.

The reaction to Peter's account was first a silencing of the opposition. There was nothing that they could gainsay. We know, however, from the subsequent struggle over this problem that it was a long time before the opposition was really quieted. Such are the ways of provincialism and prejudice. Some among them, at least, had the grace to glorify God that the kingdom had been broadened to include the Gentiles.

One question now remained for the whole Christian church and that was whether Cornelius and his people were to be regarded as exceptional cases or was the church really to be open to Gentiles. Conservatism is bound to find many intermediate stopping places. One can almost hear the opposition exclaim, "It is true, Peter, that God has accepted an outstanding man like Cornelius and the Holy Spirit has fallen upon him and his group, but you don't mean to tell us that on the basis of that we are to go out and deliberately open the doors of the church to every rag-tag pagan we find!" The struggle was far from over.

One further step toward opening the gates to the Gentiles was the unauthorized work of a number of unnamed Hellenists driven out of Jerusalem by the persecution arising over Stephen. They were good Jewish Christians and at first proclaimed the message only to other Jews as they proceeded up the coast and out to the islands. But some of them, Africans and Islanders (men of Cyprus and Cyrene, Acts 11:20), when they reached Antioch preached the Lord Jesus to Greeks, that is Gentiles, as well. No one had told them to do so. No one had told them not to. They were led by the Spirit to do it. After all, it seemed the first interracial Christian church was started at Antioch. Antioch was on the Orontes, chief city of Syria and third city of the whole Roman Empire, crossroads of east and west.

We know something about this church both from Acts

and from an incident related in Galatians. Several things of importance stand out. One is that the interracial, intercultural fellowship was new and important enough to merit an apostolic deputation. Big-hearted Barnabas, a Hellenist Christian himself from Cyprus, was sent. Galatians speaks of Peter's presence there as well, along with Barnabas. So apparently Jerusalem was much concerned with this thriving, daring experiment in Christianity. Another thing is that the Antioch church, judging by both Acts and Galatians, not only had a lively fellowship and witness of the Spirit but provided a meeting ground for discussions of this very Jew-Gentile issue. It was here that the debates arose that led to the great council of Jerusalem (Acts 15) and it is here that Paul rebuked Peter to his face for compromising on the Gentile issue and almost splitting the church (Gal. 2:11ff). It was here at Antioch (Acts 11:26) that the disciples were for the first time called "Christians." There may be no direct connection between the interracial character of the church and its taking to itself the name Christian, but the two go gloriously together.

As Christians have been discovering over the whole world and need more vigorously yet to discover, the true body of Christ is affirmed not in our sameness and cliquish similarities but across our human differences. It is precisely in those areas of difference in which not our likes and dislikes, not our egocentric whims, but the grace of God is allowed to operate and to rebuke our selfish tastes that God is able to make of diverse people one body in Christ who died for all.

Whenever any two persons get together there are bound to be differences of tastes, temperaments, and habits, whether the two be the closest of friends, husband or wife, or two casual acquaintances. There are also separate wills, unique and demanding, each individual the center of a whole universe. People who gather about them only

54

those who confirm their own opinions or reflect or echo their own biases are making a god of their own desires. What Peter was gradually beginning to learn, what Barnabas was helping to discover, what the unnamed founders and participants of the Antioch church were finding out in the crucible of human difference, and what Paul was later to forge into a theological point of view is that the divine Spirit creates for himself the body of Christ out of all the diversities of human personality. As he welds them together in love and direction he still leaves them free and creative enough to express individuality and colorful differences. In this body the differences that are trivial are overlooked, those that are detrimental are overcome, and those that are beneficial are woven into a pattern of strength and beauty. Such was the challenge of the Gentile world as the church faced it in the first century.

We are not prepared to go any further in our understanding of the early church without stopping here and taking into consideration a man whose name has of necessity crept into the story again and again, Mr. Worldwide Christian himself, Saul of Tarsus better known to us by his Roman name Paulus, or just Paul. The conversion of Saul is woven into the fabric of Acts back in chapter nine between the evangelistic exploits of the Hellenist Philip and the journeys of the apostle Peter. The thrilling story of his conversion from arch persecutor to arch preacher of the faith is retold twice in later chapters of the book (Acts 22:2-21 and 26:9-23) making it a thrice-told tale, the most fully repeated story in the book, rivaled only by the Cornelius story for repetition and emphasis.

What is the meaning of that conversion for our chapter on the Gentile challenge? Precisely this, that it was this man more than any other who epitomized in his person and his work the whole mission of Christianity to the Gentiles. According to Acts and the second chapter of Galatians, Saul was converted and commissioned at one and the same time, and the type of Christianity to which he was converted was for all the world on equal terms. Brought up a Jew of the strictest sort, he knew and appreciated well the advantages of Judaism, yet when he became a Christian he saw clearly that in the gospel of Christ there could be no second-class citizens. Jew and Gentile are both admitted on the same basis or not at all. This basis is not that of goodness or achievement for then gradations and preferments would arise, but on the basis of God's gracious gift in Christ and man's humble acceptance of the same in faith.

We shall be saying much in the coming chapters about this man Saul-Paul. No story of the early church would be complete without him. But let it be noted here that for him there is only one gospel: the gospel of God's grace available by faith to all people of every racial, natural, cultural, and religious background on an equal basis. To trace his exposition of this gospel through his great epistles to the Galatians and the Romans would take us far afield from our present objective, but we can note and be thankful that after many years of soul-searching struggle, his view finally won out. As a consequence you and I today, of whatever nationality or race, can know within ourselves as Christians that we are on equal terms before God and men. This is true in spite of the gap between the gospel as demonstrated in Christ and his church, and the gospel as reflected in the thoughts, words and deeds of many of those who claim to be his followers.

Self-centeredness, prejudice, pride, and bigotry are everyone's problems. No class or group has a monopoly on them. The important thing for us Christians is to recognize it as our problem too, and find the authentic meaning of the church for our day, affirming the true body of Christ across, around, through, and beyond all our differences.

6

The Church Faces the Complex Roman World

NOT UNTIL THE church could shake off its provincialism and have both the spirit and incentive to confront the civilization about it could there be anything like the "Church Facing the Complex Roman World."

In terms of the Book of Acts, we are now at the great continental divide, the new beginning in chapter thirteen. There are other divisions in the book but none is more important than this. Up to this point Luke has been sketching, sometimes in broad summary form, sometimes by representative stories, the birth and growth of the church in Jerusalem and its thrusts into adjacent territories. Now with chapter thirteen he seems to abandon this more general approach and takes one definite line of expansion of the church to the northwest from Antioch through Asia Minor and Greece to Rome. Great expansions of the church to the east of Antioch over into Mesopotamia, the foundations of the great Assyrian church, are not even mentioned. Nor is anything said about the rapid and substantial growth of the church to the south into Alexandria and across North Africa, for centuries to come one of the most vigorous and creative areas of the church. Not only does he select one specific direction but from this time forward he tells the story as though looking over the shoulder of one man, Saul-Paul. Since our primary purpose is to gain an understanding of the early church as a whole rather than follow the exploits of key individuals, we shall have to make a conscious effort to take the deeds of individuals simply as representative of greater issues in which the church was involved.

First then, let us take our bearings at the beginning of the thirteenth chapter of Acts, discovering the approximate time in the first century we are talking about and the extent of time that has elapsed since the resurrection of Christ. Working forward from the fixed date of AD 44 for the death of Herod Agrippa (Acts 12) and working back from the date of 51-52 for the proconsulship of Gallio in Achaia (Corinth) (Acts 18), we arrive at a time around AD 47-48 for the missionary journey of Barnabas and Saul. This means that some eighteen years have gone by since the Day of Pentecost, a passage of time almost totally unmarked by Luke. He had been intent upon the series of incidents which paint the picture of the meaning and importance of the early church and its Spirit-directed gospel. In these eighteen years the youthful, vibrant movement had spread into literally hundreds of localities and its members numbered in the tens of thousands. Christians had no doubt reached distant places and far corners of the Empire. Just a year or so later, in AD 49, an edict of the Emperor Claudius expelled Jews from Rome. There is some evidence of the presence of Christians in the capital of the Empire. Among them were Aquila and Priscilla, later to enter our story. Here we are then in 47/48 in the midstream of a growing movement of Christians beginning to infiltrate the vast Roman Empire.

It may be thought unfortunate that so much of our information about the church of this period centers on the one individual Paul, exciting and creative though he is. On the other hand, the colorful and varied experiences of Paul and his companions furnish us much information about the impact of the total church upon the diverse aspects of the Roman world.

In the last chapter we mentioned the conversion of Saul to a worldwide concept of the gospel. Contrary to a very widespread misconception among ministers and teachers, his name was not changed to Paul upon conversion. The author of Acts called him Saul until some thirteen years after his conversion, and at an appropriate point in the story introduced his Roman name Paulus. He probably had the name Paulus from birth. Every Roman citizen possessed three names and Paulus was likely his cognomen or last name.

Following his conversion, Saul spent some time around Damascus, including a period in Arabia. He made a short visit to Jerusalem and under pressure of opposition was sent off to his home city of Tarsus in Cilicia. There he spent some ten to twelve years about which we know nothing, a sharp reminder that there must be much about the great apostle of which we today are totally ignorant. Years later after the intercultural and interracial church at Antioch was getting started, Barnabas, who had welcomed and somewhat sponsored Saul at Jerusalem years before, journeyed over to Tarsus and brought him to Antioch. Barnabas must have felt that Saul would enjoy and could contribute greatly to the kind of intercultural fellowship found at Antioch. Saul worked there for some time, at one point making a trip along with Barnabas up to Jerusalem to take relief to the poverty-stricken Jerusalem church (Acts 11:29f; 12:25).

Saul was one of the five leaders of the Antioch church. In the course of time God's Holy Spirit, constantly leading his church, directed the congregation to consecrate Barnabas and Saul for the work to which he had called them, a work of further penetration into Roman society. So began what we usually call Paul's first missionary journey. In view of the ten to twelve years of Paul's work around Tarsus and the province of Cilicia about which we are ignorant, we should exercise caution in numbering too exactly what Acts leaves unspecified. We could call it his first recorded missionary journey. The total story of this journey is of interest to every student and teacher of the Bible, but for our purpose of understanding the early church we shall concentrate primarily on those aspects of Roman life and culture confronted by the gospel.

First let us look in on the court of Sergius Paulus, chief administrator of Cyprus with his capital at Paphos at the western end of the island. Paphos was largely known at this time as the center of the worship of Venus or Aphrodite, the goddess of love, and had a wide reputation for immorality. Governmentally, the island of Cyprus was under the control of the Roman Senate and its ruler was known as proconsul, as he is accurately called in Acts. Little is known of Sergius Paulus, though some identify him with a person by the same name mentioned by Pliny as a writer of natural history. Luke wrote of him as "a man of intelligence" (Acts 13:7). Since it was the custom for a Roman nobleman to have attached to his household some philosopher or soothsayer as a sort of domestic chaplain, it is not surprising to find in his employ the magician Elymas. It was also the custom for many philosophers, moralists, and religious propagandists to travel about from city to city and give public lectures. When Sergius Paulus heard of Barnabas and Saul, he probably thought of them in this light and summoned them to give a declamation before his court. The church, through two of its more daring representatives, came face to face with Roman aristocracy in the sophisticated setting of a proconsul's court.

Luke gives us no summary of Paul's message to the Roman ruler. The whole emphasis is upon the effect of the message, the conflict in the mind of the proconsul, and the dramatic clash between Paul and the court magician. Luke was concerned to let us know that it was not just an approving nod from a Roman official that was at stake, but his total life commitment. The contest was fought to the finish by the protagonists, Elymas and Paul, both of whom were of Jewish background struggling for the soul of a Roman. Paul apparently presented his case first and Elymas disputed him, giving his own interpretation of the story of Christ. With something of the directness that the apostle Peter earlier used on the Samaritan sorcerer, Paul confronted the magician to his face and pronounced him an enemy of the Lord. As proof, he declared that the hand of the Lord was upon him to strike him blind; the man was temporarily cast into darkness. Whatever persuasive arguments Paul may have used in his main presentation, it was his word-with-power that really convinced the proconsul that Paul's way was the truth and the other false.

Judged on the level of a human argument, it would seem that Paul won his case by attacking the man personally. Viewed as Acts does from the perspective of the eternal purposes of God, there was a dramatic victory of the Word of God over the widespread magic, sorcery, and superstition so prevalent in Roman society. It becomes, then, but one in a series of stories in Acts showing the supremacy of the true Spirit of God over the false spirits of the age. In addition to the Simon Magus story, note also along this line the frustrating of the profiteers with the soothsaying girl at Philippi (Acts 16:18) and the overpowering of the sons of Sceva (Acts 19:19).

Sergius Paulus, the Roman proconsul of high rank, became a believer and Saul, hitherto called by his Hebrew name, is now known by his Roman cognomen, Paulus, identical with that of the ruling officer. Not only that, but here Paul seems to have won his spurs as a missionary. From this time on it was no longer Barnabas and Saul but Paul and Barnabas in that order.

The next example of the impact of the church upon complex Roman society happened on the mainland of what we today call Asia Minor, in a territory called Pisidia. The presence of two Antiochs so close together in the story in Acts is a bit confusing. Antioch of Pisidia is the lesser known of the two. Augustus had made it a Roman colony and like Philippi it had a Latin constitution, Latin magistrates, and Latin as its official language. It supported a fairly strong Roman population, descendants of the veterans of Roman wars who had been settled there. It had its own Roman amphitheater. In fact, in this one city could be seen (1) a substratum of Phrygian culture and population, (2) overlain by the ordinary features of Greek civilization, and (3) Romanization since the time of Augustus, and (4) in its very midst a Jewish colony over 225 years old.

As so often happened throughout the empire, the impact of the church in Pisidian Antioch began with the Jewish synagogue. Luke considered it important to give us a resume of Paul's approach to these Jews of the Dispersion. Actually, Paul worked in many similar synagogues on Cyprus before coming to Antioch. Right from the opening lines of the speech (Acts 13:16 and again in 13:26) Paul addressed his hearers as two groups, the true descendants of Abraham and Gentiles who had attached themselves as inquirers into the Jewish faith, the "God-fearers." Beginning with the mighty acts of God in the Exodus, the wilderness wanderings, and the occupation of Caanan, Paul passed on to David and from him to his lineal descendant, Jesus the Savior, whom the inhabitants of Jerusalem asked the Romans to kill but whom God raised from the dead and through whom God offers salvation. This salvation he interpreted in terms of freedom "from everything from which you could not be freed by the law of Moses" (Acts 13:39). After the first sermon the people asked for more such preaching the next sabbath and many, both among the Jews and proselytes, became believers. The crowd the following sabbath was greater than ever and the opposition tougher, precipitating an open clash. Then, in what became a familiar pattern from this time on, the Christian preachers declared that the gospel had to be preached first to the Jews to give them as the people of God the first chance, but because they refused it, "judging themselves unworthy of eternal life," the gospel would be presented to the Gentiles. They quoted one of the Isaiah servant texts to which we referred in the Pentecost story about "a light for the Gentiles" and "salvation to the uttermost parts of the earth." So the Gentiles, both the basic Phrygian stock and the Greeks and Romans and all mixtures in between, were not only given a chance but responded joyfully and in large numbers. But the apostles' success proved also their undoing. Success brought crowds, and crowds either aroused jealousy or gave the appearance of tumult. In either case the result was reprisal and finally expulsion. No doubt there were Romans among the new Christian believers. The opponents of the gospel succeed in stirring up the Roman aristocracy of the city against them. The "leading men" were a group of Roman nobles called the *duumviri,* the board of magistrates who ruled the city. These city leaders were in turn pressured by the women of high standing who apparently were attached to the synagogue. By this time the apostles had a thriving new church going, so did not regret shaking off the dust of their feet and moving on to Iconium.

A similar uprising happened at Iconium, only the violence was even more intense with attempts, by various types of people including Roman leaders again, at outright violence. This kind of rough treatment followed them to the next town as well where opponents from both Antioch and Iconium incited the people to stone Paul.

Thus far the impact of the church on complex Roman society has been illustrated largely in terms of the nobility: the aristocratic proconsul of Cyprus and his court who were sympathetic, and the city magistrates of Antioch and Iconium who demonstrated something of Roman ruthlessness. At the next town, Lystra, there was yet another aspect of Roman civilization to cope with.

Lystra, like Antioch, had been made a Roman colony by Augustus and was connected with Antioch by an imperial road. It too had some veterans of the Roman wars among its earlier inhabitants. But the Romans seemed to be much more in the minority in this smaller, more primitive town. The predominant element was the old Lycaonian stock, still speaking the old dialect and showing a less sophisticated, less cynical attitude toward the worship of the gods. True, the ancient sanctuary was by now remodeled and dedicated to Zeus known as "Zeus-before-the-city," because his shrine was outside the town. If there were a scarcity of true Romans in the town, there was also a scarcity of Jews. In fact, there were not the ten male Jews required to found a synagogue so Paul and company preached as best they could in the streets.

It is difficult to know whether Paul would have made much headway among the primitive Lycaonians had it not been for a remarkable cure of a man crippled from birth. Through faith and at the command of Paul this hopeless man leaped up and walked (Acts 14:10). Now the ice was broken. People immediately took notice and their first reaction was that the ancient gods had come down among them in the persons of Paul and Barnabas. In the superstitious mind of the primitives of this town the sky hung low and the gods readily walked the earth with men. Barnabas, perhaps a patriarchal figure with impressive stature, was called Zeus the father of the gods, and Paul, the spokesman of the team, was Hermes his messenger. It was apparently some time before Paul and Barnabas sensed what was going on. When, however, they saw the priest of the temple of Zeus-before-the-city bringing oxen bedecked with garlands in the act of offering sacrifice to them, the apostles finally realized their situation and, Hebrews that they were, they rent their garments in holy horror. If the cynicism of some Romans bothered them, the superstitions of these old-fashioned polytheists completely astounded them.

Rushing out into the crowd they cried out in *koine* Greek, the language which the priests also knew, and tried to stop them. Instead of gods, they shouted, they were men like themselves. They were ordinary men but they brought an extraordinary message, the good news from heaven of a God who has not left himself without a witness in any culture. Nothing more is said of their message, but apparently at some time or other they had opportunity to present the whole gospel, for a church was begun at Lystra, this strangely primitive town on one of the imperial roads of the Roman empire.

The ending of the visit to Lystra is as dramatic as its beginning. One day people were hailing Paul and Barnabas as gods. A few days later they were taking up stones and pelting them. Maybe the same people were not doing both, but it is the same town, the same culture, and elements in the same society. For determined enemies of the gospel had arrived from Antioch and Iconium, and stirred up the volatile Galatians. (Lystra is located in the southern part of the Roman province by that name.) This time they almost made an end of all Paul's travels. His first missionary journey almost became his last — but not quite. God who authorized and inspired this journey was looking after Paul.

We have seen three examples of the impact of the early church upon diverse facets of the mighty Roman empire and its mixed and varied culture. What can we say in summary of this witness as far as we have noted it? The Christians went right ahead with vigor and forthrightness and proclaimed the gospel to the Romans as they would to anyone else, sowing the seed and letting God give the increase. This is true of authentic missionary work in any culture. Secondly we can say that since the Roman empire embraced such a motley mixture of types and elements (like American culture today) most any kind of response might be expected. Some Romans were disillusioned by their former philosophies and religions and were hungry for something that met their deepest needs. Men like Cornelius of Caesarea the Roman army officer, Sergius Paulus the proconsul of Cyprus, and scores of other unnamed people were among them. Certainly one should observe about Roman society, mixed and varied as it was, that the response the church might receive would cover the whole spectrum, from the joyous acceptance of the Gentile believers at Pisidian Antioch who "were glad and glorified the word of God" to the bitter opposition of the determined residents of the same Antioch who persecuted the missionaries of the faith from town to town. There would be everything from the scornful cynicism of an Elymas to the fickle idolatry of the Lycaonians. But there would also be the acceptance of a mature and intelligent man like Sergius and the trusting discipleship of others like Timothy, convert from Lystra.

We shall have the Romans with us from this time on in the story as we consider other aspects of the continually growing and expanding church.

7

The Church and Unity Through Diversity

WE SAID IN AN earlier chapter that the Gentile problem
was not quickly solved. Attitudes which are born of centuries of deep-seated prejudice and protected by taboos
and feelings that lie buried within one's personality are
not easily resolved. Witness, for example, the race issue
in our own country: the long years of struggle and sacrifice that have already gone into achieving the measure of
progress we have seen and the years of further sacrifice
and struggle that lie ahead.

In this chapter we shall study one of the milestones
along the road in meeting the Gentile challenge. This
milestone was not the end of the problem by any means,
but it provides us an excellent place to observe close up
the problem of unity through diversity in the life of the
church. The consultation held in Jerusalem and recorded
in Acts 15, the first recorded conference in the history of
the church, has served as a precedent and model for church

conferences and councils ever since. It is important, then, that we go into it with as much thoroughness as is possible within the scope of these pages.

The first step in the drama is one which we covered in part as we considered the first recorded missionary journey of Paul and Barnabas. These Christian missionaries took Gentiles into the church without requiring the Gentiles to become Jews first and then Christians. Whenever there were Jews present, Paul and Barnabas would give them the first opportunity as the people of God to come into the Kingdom of their Messiah. Jews who came were welcomed and formed part of the nucleus of the new Christian church. A number of the Jewish Christians in Macedonia and Achaia (provinces in Greece) are mentioned by name in the Bible. But when the majority of Jews refused the gospel, as they did eventually in every known instance, Paul and Barnabas would turn to the Gentiles. Also in localities where there was no synagogue, as at Lystra, the apostles would take the message at once to the Gentiles. They did not require the Gentiles to undergo the Jewish rite of circumcision, but took them in directly.

Opening the door to Gentiles without the requirements of the law appeared to be a very dangerous policy in the opinion of the more conservative Christians of Jerusalem. Unfortunately, we do not have any of their arguments preserved for us but we can imagine some which they might have used. For example, one of them might have said:

> God gave the law to Moses and it was meant to be followed. Until God himself releases us from it we are bound to go on following it. A liberal like Paul will destroy the whole people of God.

And another might have rejoined:

> Our Lord himself kept the law during his earthly life; he himself was circumcised the eighth day according

to the law and never do we hear of him teaching us to break with it except where it conflicts with human need.

Then still another might have added:

> Not only was Jesus circumcised, and we are supposed to be like him, but so were all the early disciples and apostles of the Lord. In fact, up until these modern trends set in, all Christians have been good Jews. Even Paul himself who advocates these dangerous practices is a circumcised Jew.

Reason, logic, and the weight of religious tradition all seemed to be on the conservative side. Therefore, it is with some weight and certainty that "some men came down from Judea [apparently to Antioch] and were teaching the brethren, 'Unless you are circumcised according to the custom of Moses, you cannot be saved.'"

Despite the reason, the logic, and the weight of religious tradition, Paul and Barnabas did not agree with them and as a result had considerable "dissension and debate" about the matter ("fierce dissension and controversy," as the New English Bible calls it). The difference of opinion was sharp, forthright, and honest on both sides. What should the church do? As in the case of the dissension over the Hellenists and their widows, the wiser leadership of the church was determined not to let this serious problem upset or split the church. Paul, Barnabas, and some of the others were appointed by the Antioch church, apparently, to go up to Jerusalem and consult with the apostles and elders about the matter — in other words, hold a conference on it. It was not to be a conference to which the congregations or districts would send delegates, but a council of concern in which various parties to the dispute would be represented and all would have an opportunity to present their points of view.

This does not mean, however, that this was to be a

parliamentary meeting decided strictly by human considerations and majority rule. God is sovereign, not his human subjects. His Spirit directs the church in all its decisions, and his will must be sought through all consultations. We shall note the frequent mention of God's initiative, God's direction, and God's will in the decision. A purely humanistic reading here would distort the true meaning of this account just as much as it would in Acts 2 or any other part of this book.

It is interesting to note the activity of Paul and Barnabas on the way to the conference. Beginning at Antioch in Syria they journeyed through Phoenicia and Samaria, both areas by this time liberally sprinkled with Christian groups; and everywhere they went they related the missionary experiences they had had among the Gentiles. They witnessed to everyone what God had done through them to open a door of faith to the Gentiles. According to the way God had been leading them and directing their work, there was no question in their minds as to his will on the issue to be debated at the conference.

At Jerusalem also, Paul and Barnabas were well-received and had a chance to tell their exciting story. But the opposition, "believers who belonged to the party of the Pharisees," also had their say and came back at them insistently with their requirement for all Gentile Christians: "It is necessary to circumcise them, and to charge them to keep the law of Moses."

As so often in Acts, we are not let in on what would be the most interesting details of the conference, the personal infighting, the arguments used on both sides, just who got angry and walked out, and so forth. If Galatians 2 is a description of this same council, and this is perhaps the best reading of that passage, there were some very tense moments, with, as Paul puts it, some "false brethren secretly brought in . . . to spy out our freedom . . . in Christ Jesus that they might bring us into bondage."

There was Paul's refusal to "yield submission even for a moment that the truth of the gospel might be preserved" for all his converts, past and future (Gal. 2:1-5). Acts simply says there was "much debate" and then goes on to report a speech by Peter in which he recalled the first case of Gentiles being admitted into the church. Peter told how God bore witness to all present at the house of Cornelius by pouring out his Holy Spirit on them as on the Day of Pentecost, "making no distinction between us [Jews] and them [as Gentiles] but cleansed their hearts by faith." Then turning directly to the opposition, Peter accused them of "provoking" God, as the New English Bible renders it (literally "making trial of" him or "tempting" him), by putting a yoke upon the neck of their Gentile converts "which neither our fathers nor we have been able to bear." Peter meant not only the yoke of keeping the law, but deeper yet, the implicit necessity of earning one's salvation by law observance. Then he made a statement which sounds very much like that which Paul told Peter at Antioch (Gal. 2:16ff): it is by the grace of the Lord Jesus, not our keeping of the law, that Jewish Christians are saved and it is by this grace also that Gentiles are saved.

Though spoken by Peter, this would have been the answer of Paul and Barnabas to their conservative group. Paul would have agreed, in effect, that granted their basic premise, the logic and reason and weight of religious tradition was on their side. But their major premise was all wrong. We do not earn our way into the favor of God. No man can be saved by his good works, even the good works of obedience to the law of God. Man always falls short and it is only by the grace of God that any one, be he Jew or Gentile, is saved.

Anyone wishing a much more complete exposition of this should read Paul's letter to the Romans, particularly the first four chapters. The good works come after the act of being made right, "justification" as it is called. One should read on through the remainder of the book of Romans, especially from chapter twelve on, and discover the place and necessity of doing good as the fruit, not the root of salvation.

Peter made the crucial speech. In the Cornelius episode, which Peter recalled, and in the truth that divine grace is the only way to salvation there was too much evidence of divine working for anyone to dispute his case. The opposition was hushed. Barnabas and Paul then, as the story goes, had another chance to tell of the signs and wonders God had done through them among the Gentiles. Then finally, James, the elder of the Jerusalem church and apparently moderator of the meeting, made the summarizing speech. James was known as a conservative himself. The circumcision party had used his name as their authority, according to Paul (Gal. 2:11). So when he spoke he had the ear, if not the total backing, of the conservative group.

In the summary Luke gives of his speech, James echoed pretty much the point of view expressed by Peter, quoting freely from the prophets to back up God's call of the Gentiles. He then suggested that they not further burden the Gentiles who became Christians, at least not require them to keep the whole Jewish law, but simply instruct them to avoid some of the more abhorrent features of Gentile life. One of these was idolatry and pollution by idols. Some of the best meat to be had in some cities (Corinth for example) was meat sold around the idol temples. Many broadminded Christians of Gentile background saw nothing wrong in continuing this shopping and eating habit. The Christians were also asked to keep away from involvement in the great amount of sexual immorality associated with pagan life. This was prevalent not only around the same idol temples but in general in the life of society about them. The third area

James mentioned had to do with diet again, the avoidance of meats not properly butchered or bled. For the good Jew, life is sacred unto the Lord and the life is in the blood. It must not be eaten.

In one sense this proposal was a compromise. The great mission to the Gentiles could go on. One misses from James' carefully chosen words, however, very much enthusiasm for going out and making more and more converts. He simply spoke against troubling those who do turn to God. He seemed to ignore Paul and Barnabas altogether. Nor did he deal with the very important issue of salvation by grace rather than by law, which we have seen was really the heart of the matter and the one basic answer to the conservative position.

Maybe this was more than a diplomatic compromise. Perhaps it was intended to mean that James was conceding that Paul and Barnabas were in the right. If the elder of the Jerusalem church had been as conservative as Paul pictured him (Gal. 2) and as our knowledge of his reputation among the Jews as James the Just, we may have here the statement of a man who was being gradually won over by the work of God among the Gentiles through men like these who had spoken. In other words, he could not, in the face of the evidence "withstand God," to use Peter's wording as he reported his Cornelius incident to Jerusalem. We are no doubt correct in seeing James as one of the elders to whom Peter had reported on that memorable occasion when he had been called on to explain his actions in the Cornelius case (Acts 11:1-18) and now that incident bears fruit.

If we are correct, and James himself was being won over to a more liberal position, slowly and perhaps a bit reluctantly, then his concession would tend to settle the matter, meaning that the case of the strict circumcision party was lost. Peter, Paul, and Barnabas won, if not complete endorsement, at least considerable encouragement. It is interesting to note in this connection that the letter compiled by the council to be sent as the official answer to the original query went much further than James did, first by condemning the conservatives as trouble-makers, unsettling the minds of the people entirely without authorization from Jerusalem, and then by praising "our beloved Barnabas and Paul, men who have risked their lives for the sake of our Lord Jesus Christ." Evidence that this was really the Holy Spirit's work is seen in the willingness of a staunch conservative like James to come as far as he did in approving the reception of Gentiles without circumcision. Further evidence is in the more hearty endorsement of the whole mission to the Gentiles contained in this official statement of the conference.

An aspect of considerable importance is the fact that the council not only composed a letter giving what to them was the divine will ("it has seemed good to the Holy Spirit and to us" as they put it), but commissioned two men of standing, Silas and Judas Barsabbas, to be the personal bearers of the letter and to interpret it to the people and answer all questions. These men were prophets or preachers in their own right who were able to make a real contribution to the churches of the Gentile frontier like Antioch and other parts of Syria and Cilicia.

Seen, then, in the light of the total life of the ongoing church, the conference at Jerusalem was a great experience in preserving church unity in and through diversity of opinion. The issue could easily have split the church into two factions: one conservative, sectarian, pro-Jewish, too fettered by national and cultural restrictions to have carried forward the mission to the whole world, and the other broad enough to take in Gentiles but in danger of being cut loose from the historical past and therefore liable to adulteration or syncretism, or of going the way of the mystery religions of the day.

What Luke was trying to tell us, it would seem, is that when faced by a real problem which might have divided the church, the Christians sent their most dedicated leaders to meet and confer and to pray for divine guidance. Out of this came a working basis for unity through diversity.

This unity would not outlaw all diversity, that is, impose an absolute uniformity. The church continued to have freedom and spontaneity, and never permitted itself to be tied to one form or one monolithic structure, either of organization or doctrine. This would have been to attempt to trap the Holy Spirit of God in straight jackets of human origin and in the end would have meant the strangulation of the very unity it was expected to promote.

This was not unity along with diversity, as though there were two equal values, unity and diversity which, like the lion and the lamb, should lie down together. While such a mixture might last a while, one suspects that the final state would be one in which either the unity would be so impaired by its unrelated diversity that it would cease to exist, or the diversity so out of step with any true concept of unity that it would turn to chaos. Such a situation, a house divided, could not long stand.

Nor, again, was this a unity to be achieved in spite of diversity, as though diversity in itself was wrong and that man at his best was meant to be uniform in thought and action. Such a concept would be sure to misunderstand and eventually stifle or stamp out all human freedom and end up as a dead conformity.

No, the unity of the early church, while far from perfect even as the members of that church were far from perfect, was a unity in and through diversity. Diversity, like spontaneity, was not only allowed to exist, but was regarded as glorious expressions of a free and sovereign God. Therefore the diversities of viewpoint and expression, held together by a solid commitment to one Lord, one faith and one baptism (perhaps not one form or formula of baptism, but one baptism), were actually evidences of this higher unity of the Spirit. In the creative diversity of such a church there was proof that this was not the product of some dictatorial human mind or will, seeking to superimpose itself upon a society and demand conformity. It was proof that here were persons, created in the image of God to be free but not rebellious, creative but not chaotic, spontaneous but not undisciplined. This meant that under God in Christ members in the church could give and take rebuke, could engage in free and sometimes sharp debate precisely because they were bound together in a community which was not of their own making but was the gift of God. They could agree to differ and yet stay together until they should discover the will of God through their differences.

Judas and Silas, the men commissioned to carry the decision of the conference, were the living spokesmen for the unity of the church by which they were appointed. They went about among the congregations reading the letter and adding their own personal weight and testimony to it. Then in the course of time, when Paul found himself without his former teammate Barnabas (due to some real diversity of opinion of their own over John Mark), Paul took one of these council representatives, Silas, as his partner and set off on another journey, this one longer and more eventful than the first.

In trying to assess the total effect of the Council of Jerusalem we must say again that it did not mean the end of the Gentile problem so far as the church was concerned. Think of how many conferences in our own day have made pronouncements about peace and war and remember in what virulent form the problem is still with us, or think of the conferences which have declared the unity and equality of the races in the sight of God and think how the race problem still persists! A conference may not of itself, either through its resolutions, its representatives, or its general influence, solve a problem. It can be an affirmation, indeed a symbol, of the solution which it can espouse but which only God can eventually effect. The Gentile problem persisted on in the early church for a number of years, cropping up here and there in one form or another. To its continuation we owe, in part at least, two of Paul's most effective writings: Galatians, sometimes called the "Magna Charta of Christian Freedom" and Romans, the most complete statement we have of both his theology and his ethics. But the Council of Jerusalem stands as a sort of monument to the solution which finally came, freeing the church for centuries to come from second-class citizenship for its Gentile members which would have been a perpetual negation of the Spirit of Christ. Regretfully other forms of dual or multiple citizenships still exist (first-class, second-class and sometimes third-class) both in and out of the church with respect to race, nationality, social and economic class. But the possibility of unity here also, as with the Jew-Gentile question, comes not in violation of, in spite of, nor along side of diversity, but directly in and through diversity. This has already been shown and made monumental through the Jerusalem Conference and in the literature of Paul.

8

The Church and the Greeks

FOR SOME TIME now in our study of the early church as
depicted in the Book of Acts we have been working
away at one of the major concerns in the book, namely
the way in which the Christian message was carried to
people of various cultures. It should be understood, right
from the start, that in the view of Acts, the essential witness of the church was the same to all and there was no
hedging or compromising at that point. On the other
hand, there was a recognition of the fact that not only are
people individuals with differences of temperament and
taste, but they are set in cultural streams which influence
and condition their thinking. As the gospel was presented
to persons in different cultures it was likely to meet with
different responses as conditioned, in part at least, by
those cultures.

One of the cultures which underlay the Roman empire was the Hellenic or Greek. It was already in a period

of decadence but its language, ways of thinking and acting, as well as the legacy of its literature and art lived on. The church came into localities deeply influenced with Greek culture and we wish to consider this in the next two chapters. We shall concentrate in this chapter on those aspects of the impact upon Greek culture which were not peculiarly urban in nature.

On what we call the second missionary journey, Paul, Silas, and Timothy from Lystra journeyed from Antioch of Syria across Galatia, across the corner of the province of Asia, and on to Troas. There Paul received the well-known "Macedonian Call" and crossed over into that province. The cities in which he and his assistants worked, as noted in Acts, were Philippi, Thessalonica, and Beroea. These were cities largely populated by Macedonian Greeks, but the amount of information given us by Acts as to the impact of the gospel upon the Greek mind there is relatively meager. The major incidents in Philippi had to do with the exploiters of a soothsaying girl, the Roman magistrates by whom Paul was illegally flogged, and a Roman jailer. In Thessalonica most of the action was initiated by Paul's Jewish opponents who stirred up the volatile mob hanging around that seaport city and ran him out of town. In Beroea the very brief stay revolved largely around Jews again, these more "noble" than those at Thessalonica by virtue of their daily search of the Scriptures. We gain considerably more understanding of the problems raised by the Greek mind about Christianity when we read the correspondence Paul had with converts in Macedonia, notably at Thessalonica and Philippi.

Reading between the lines of the Thessalonian letters we discover two problems in particular which arose out of aspects of the Greek culture of the time. The first of these was the widespread laxity in sexual morality and marriage. In First Thessalonians the very first item Paul discusses in the section on church problems (chapters four and five) is this one. As Christians they are to "abstain from immorality." Each one is to "know how to take a wife for himself in holiness and honor and not in the passion of lust like heathen who do not know God." No one is to "wrong his brother in this matter." Apparently promiscuity across marital lines was common in the culture about them and was even invading the church, so that Paul was both explicit and strong in his rebuke: "The Lord is an avenger in all these things . . . God has not called us for uncleanness, but in holiness . . . and whoever disregards this, disregards not man but God." Likewise at Corinth, notorious even among the pagans for its immorality, the new Christian fellowship was constantly imperiled by both the threat and the presence of sexual and marital problems.

The second problem dealt with in the letters to Macedonia which sprang quite naturally out of the Greek mind and culture was a tendency toward excessive individualism and divisiveness. From the time of Greek city-states on down, freedom of thought and action had been one of the cherished ideals of the Greeks. Like the Americans of today the Greeks talked a great deal about freedom. The difficulty arises when this freedom becomes individualistic and divisive. Any reader of ancient Greek history will remember that one of the distressing aspects of their political life was their lack of cohesiveness and the almost constant civil wars among the Greeks themselves. It was part of their culture to think and do as they pleased; as a result pride and provincialism often stood in the way of a higher unity. All the surviving letters which Paul wrote to Greeks, whether of Macedonia to the north or Achaia in the south, stress the overcoming of divisiveness within the body of Christ.

At Thessalonica certain persons in the church were so convinced of their own view that the Lord was about to return that they quit working, lived off the main body of the church, and caused a great deal of talk both within and outside the fellowship. They, or others of their group, were also insubordinate so far as the leaders of the church were concerned. In Philippians being of one mind, united, and at peace is one of the dominant themes. There also, in addition to general divisiveness, two women, Euodia and Syntyche, were not getting along and had to be exhorted to find common agreement in the Lord. The divisiveness of the Corinthian church is too well-known to require discussion. What may not be so easily realized is the fact that several other problems among the Corinthians also had their origin in this same impulse to freedom without discipline and rugged individualism, for example: the behavior of the women in church, the disruption of their love feast communion services, and the tendency of members to go to law against one another.

In Acts, it is not until we come to Paul's work at Athens (recorded in Acts 17:16ff) that we see the early church really in contact with the Greek mind. Practically every line of that account is packed with meaning for us. First, Paul was impressed by the statuary he saw on every hand in Athens. It was not, however, the world-renowned beauty of this art that he noted but the fact that many of these were statues to the gods. The Greeks were, judging by their art, a very idolatrous people. It was this that gave him the basis and starting point for his famous speech in the court of the Areopagus.

In addition to arguing in the synagogue with the Jews and their circle on the sabbath, Paul took up the cause of witnessing by daily speeches in the *agora,* a kind of open forum in the market. Among his hearers there were philosophers of both the Epicurean and Stoic schools. Whatever his opinion of them, their opinion of him was not so flattering: "spermologos" they called him: "seed-picker" or spelled out in the vernacular: "chatterer, empty talker." What would this babbler say?

They listened enough to catch snatches of his speech about Jesus and *anastasis,* that is, Jesus and the resurrection. They interpreted these words as names for another pair of male and female gods, a common enough phenomenon among the mystery cults. They brought Paul to the Areopagus, the court before which murder cases were once tried, perhaps no more than a convenient forum in which to test the temper of this amateur religionist. For the Athenians were professionals, full-time inquirers into the new and different. In other words, they were educated loafers.

Paul's speech to the council is one of the best known parts of Acts and one of the most controversial. By some students of the Bible it is regarded as a model of public speaking, especially for the way in which it introduces the subject with a complimentary beginning, makes a reference to something local and visual, and then employs a clever takeoff to get into the heart of the matter. All this it has. But we miss the point if that is all we see. It is actually Luke's representation of the church confronting the Greek mind.

Other biblical scholars, however, regard the speech as so miserable a failure as to amount to nothing less than a farce. Certainly the response was not overwhelming. Luke presented it neither as a model of oratorical excellence nor as a religious failure, but as a serious witness and proclamation of the gospel in terms which the Greek mind might absorb and even accept. The response was mixed, some hearers mocking but others believing. A church of Greek converts was started, however, and the Greek Orthodox Church traces its beginning from this ministry.

What was the church's witness to Greek culture as reflected in this speech and what were the factors of vital interest involved? For one thing, in place of the Greek search for God, their feeling after the unknown (typical

82

Greek empiricism), Paul offered a gospel of divine initiative and revelation. God made the world and all that is in it, including all races of man, and is not far from any one of us. Then in place of a god to be represented in gold, silver, or stone, even in works of exquisite art, he spoke of God who is to be worshiped by repentance of the whole man. Furthermore, instead of a god caught in the trap of endless cycles of fate or a party to a vague uncertain future, he preached a God who has fixed a day on which he will judge the world in righteousness by means of the One whom he has appointed. Proof of all that Paul said about God — his divine initiative, his demand for total commitment, his firm hand upon the destiny of men and nations — is God's mighty act of raising this Man, Christ Jesus, from the dead.

The mention of the resurrection of the dead was what set some to hooting and mocking. Whether this opposition was great enough that Paul was unable to finish his speech, as some interpreters picture it, or whether this was simply all that Luke chose to give in his brief digest, we cannot be sure. There does seem to be a direct connection with these attitudes of the Greeks reflected by Paul when he wrote to the Corinthians to the effect that the cross of Christ (and in that he included the resurrection) was a stumbling block to the Jews and "folly" to the Greeks (1 Cor. 1:22).

The Greeks knew of many myths of dying and rising gods, but here was a man who seemed to believe that this sort of thing had actually happened recently and that the whole course of history was determined by it. To the prevailing Greek temper this was just too much to swallow, sheer folly, to state it mildly. Neither the detached individualism of the Epicureans nor the stern compliance with natural law of the Stoics could find any room for this sort of thing. Only a few Greeks of Athens would discover the marks of authenticity in Paul, both in his

83

moral earnestness and in the divine claims laid upon them by his preaching, and would respond in faith.

There are demonstrated in the speech itself and the responses to it several marks of the Greek mind. First, there is evident the common emphasis of the Greeks upon the empirical search for the meaning of life and of God, man's constant quest for understanding — an emphasis that is still very much with us in science and the scientific mind. Secondly, the Greek love of form and beauty and the visual representation of the best in life are strongly in evidence, another contribution of the ancient Greeks to modern civilization. A third trait of Greek thinking found here is a fatalistic uncertainty about the outcome of time and history. The cyclic or periodic view of time was very common, and the concept of a goal of history terminating in a judgment fixed by the foreknowledge of God struck them as ridiculous. A fourth tendency was not to take sin or social responsibility seriously and to regard forgiveness as either unnecessary (errors were the result of cosmic forces) or unmanly and beneath the dignity of whatever gods existed. Hence, Paul's emphasis upon repentance would strike them as all right for some unkempt itinerant Cynic philosopher, but not for respectable people. Still a fifth trait of sophisticated Greek thought represented here is a skepticism about the unseen and the supernatural. Things like resurrections happened only in the old myths which no one really took seriously. Supernatural manifestations were completely divorced from the solid facts of history and everyday life, they thought.

If we find echoes of the Greek mind still strong among us today, we need only remember that modern civilization is pretty much the product of the Renaissance which was the revival of the classical Greek philosophy, art, and empirical science. The impact of the Christian church upon the ancient Greeks, then, is virtually the story of the impact of Christianity upon our modern secular mind.

We turn now to the record of this impact as reflected in the most extensive surviving correspondence which Paul had with any one church, his Corinthian letters. Few self-respecting Greeks of that day would be happy for us to include the Corinthians in the record, for the Corinthians were regarded as degenerate. Paul himself said of the group which he was able to call together at Corinth to form a church that not many of them were wise, powerful, or of noble birth by worldly standards (1 Cor. 1:26). But since a civilization is judged not only by its best representative but by its average and even inferior products, we may turn to the hints we glean from the Corinthian correspondence as to the impact of the early church upon the Greek mind.

As we have seen, several problems already mentioned were also the problems of the Corinthian Christians: sexual immorality, a certain divisiveness and undisciplined individualism, and their intellectual difficulty with the cross and resurrection. Much more could be said about the Corinthian's difficulty with the resurrection, since a whole chapter of Paul's letter (1 Cor. 15) deals specifically with this problem. In brief their problem with the resurrection of believers was that which any Greek would raise, the complete absurdity, to the scientific mind, of a resurrection of the body when everyone knows that the body disintegrates after death. Paul's answer to this point was first a basic faith in God's resurrecting power as demonstrated in the raising of Christ and secondly, the hope of God's transformation of the physical body into a spiritual one.

A further trait of the Greek mind of the day as reflected in the Corinthian letters is a pretension of culture without the reality. The now decadent Greek civilization was living off the glories of the past. Greeks thought of themselves as the civilized men of the world and all others as barbarians. They were the heirs of the immortal philosophers, tragedians, orators, artists, and statesmen of bygone days. Their contempt of others was often ill-concealed. Even the lowborn Corinthians found Paul's manner and speech weak and disgusting. The silver-tongued Apollos matched more nearly their tastes. Their cultural pretension was reflected again and again in the kind of reply Paul must make to them, sometimes with biting sarcasm, as when he chided them for acting like kings, or in straight moral teaching when he said that "knowledge puffs up; but love builds up" (1 Cor. 8:1). To meet a crisis in personal relationships with them he resorted to the desperate tactic of boasting, though he hated himself for it. He boasted largely to hold up a mirror to them and show them what their boasting looked like (2 Cor. 10 — 13). Fortunately, this boasting along with his moral earnestness in pleading with them eventually bore fruit and brought them to their senses.

Still a final trait of some Greeks, akin no doubt to the experience many of them sought in the mystery cults of the day, was their love for ecstatic religious exercise. Such emotional expression of devotion, closely related to the doctrine of the outpoured Spirit of God, became quite a problem at Corinth. Combine their love for ecstacy with their excessive individualism and you can understand the chaos of some of the Christian meetings. Chapters twelve to fourteen of First Corinthians deal with the problem, first under the general heading of diverse spiritual gifts (chapter twelve), and then the highest gift of all — Christian love (chapter thirteen), and then specifically in terms of speaking in tongues in chapter fourteen. Alongside the well-known Greek doctrine of freedom Paul attempted to set the virtue of order or reverent decorum as a counterbalance.

The church came to the Greeks, preaching essentially the same gospel as always but meeting resistance at certain key points: sexual morality, unity and fellowship, a divinely directed view of time and history, a doctrine of the cross and resurrection (both of Christ and believers), the matter of true Christian humility, and finally, unity of the total body of Christ. The Christian answer to these objections came not only in verbal and written replies but in the costly stuff of pastoral care and long-suffering shepherding, such as Paul gave them. The results of the ministry among the Greeks, though meager at first, became in the course of time of great importance, so that from among them for several centuries were to emerge some of the greatest leaders of thought of the whole Christian church. To this day the Eastern Orthodox Church is one of the three great branches of Christianity.

The gospel came to the Greeks. The Greeks responded and are still making their contribution to the Kingdom. Furthermore, the Greek mind is still with us in the intellectual climate of our own scientific civilization.

9

The Church and the Big City

IN THE PREVIOUS CHAPTER, in considering the early church and its impact upon Greek culture we traced Paul's ministry as far as Corinth. It is our purpose now to focus our attention upon the work of the church in two important urban centers, Corinth and Ephesus. They are significant not only because of the size and influence of these cities themselves but also because of the seriousness with which the church was planted in them. It was here that Paul worked longer than in any of the cities of his travels: eighteen months at Corinth and two to three years at Ephesus.

Corinth in Paul's day was a relatively new city. The old city of Corinth, famous for its architecture and drama, was destroyed in 146 BC by the Roman general Mummius, but a hundred years later Julius Caesar had rebuilt the city as a Roman colony and made it the capital of Achaia. From its commanding location on the isthmus it soon became a boom town, a commercial center of first importance. The flow of trade brought to the city a cosmopolitan population and every conceivable religious cult. High on the hill back of the city was the temple of Aphrodite, home of two thousand sacred prostitutes. Central in the worship of the city were the rites of the Egyptian mother goddess Isis and her consort Osiris. Corinth, noted for its vice and various forms of debauchery, became a byword for immorality. Its ready access to Rome to the west and its undeniable spiritual need made it, however, a most challenging place in which to plant the Christian church. This does not mean that it was an easy spot. Quite the contrary, Paul found it right from the first one of the more difficult places for a vital Christianity to take root and flourish.

On top of a Greek substructure was a heavy overlay of Roman practices and manners. For example, Corinth was the first of the Greek cities to have a Roman amphitheater where gladiators fought to the death with men and beasts. What could the church do in the midst of such a city, the empty shell of an ancient civilization and the incarnation of some of the worst elements of the new? Paul must have questioned his ministry there many times during that year and a half — and many times more — during the long struggle to help the church after he left it. It was surely not without reason that while in Corinth he was given a vision from the Lord (Acts 18:9f), assuring him not be afraid but to speak out. There was plenty to intimidate a person in a city like Corinth. "I am with you," said the Lord, "and no man shall attack you to harm you; for I have many people in this city."

We dealt in the last chapter with the problems Paul had with the cultural pretensions, the exasperating arrogance, and the inherent divisiveness of the Greek temperament as represented at Corinth. These were tendencies of the Greek mind which Paul might have encountered almost anywhere in that part of the Empire. But our interest in this chapter is upon those aspects of the Graeco-Roman culture particularly associated with urban life.

One of these features of the urban situation was the presence on a concentrated scale of every conceivable form of idolatry. Combined with it was the difficulty Gentile Christians had of extricating themselves from this idolatry. In a small community or sparsely settled area, whatever centers of iniquity exist are well-noted by the good folk and can be more easily avoided. But a large city, ancient or modern, offers more opportunities for questionable places and practices to exist without attracting attention. And those who wish to frequent such places or indulge in such forms of vice can do so with comparative immunity from social pressure. They simply escape into the anonymity of the crowd. This is true of city life by its very nature, in whatever century or culture. The prevalence of idolatry in the large commercial city of Corinth and the close association of prostitution with idolatry made it an especially difficult place for people of "clean hands and pure hearts." Purity by avoidance was almost impossible. Even the meat you would eat in a friend's house might first have been offered to an idol or may have been purchased in a temple of iniquity. For some Corinthians this kind of situation offered no serious problem (1 Cor. 8); for others it was most serious. Church members, already divided from one another by the sheer weight of numbers which made true community next to impossible, became touchy on such matters. Paul had to labor hard by word and letter to keep alive among them true Christian brotherliness.

Similar to the contamination by pagan religious rites was the Christians' easy involvement in the pagan courts. In Corinth Christian brothers were suing one another before the law. The brokenness of urban existence often made it difficult to achieve true understanding between

Christian and Christian. Those dealing with each other might soon find themselves wrangling and quarreling and finally bringing their differences before outright pagans for settlement. This, Paul said, is defeat of essential Christianity all the way (1 Cor. 6:7). It is further a reflection of real weakness on the part of the Christian church that it would not be able to settle the petty differences that might arise among its members.

Thus at Corinth Paul faced the deeply entrenched wickedness of mass concentration of human beings and the easy contamination of the church by pagan immorality and idolatry. Coupled with this was a brokenness in community and communication that made the people suspicious and distrustful of one another, led easily to factions, and hardened brotherly relationships into quarrels and lawsuits.

What Paul did to correct these matters may be read in various passages in his Corinthian correspondence. To most of these problems there were no easy solutions — the power of God and the spirit of love, yes; but any permanent plan for solving the problems of city life, no. There is no social action program or plan of city renewal implied in either the Acts account or Paul's Corinthian correspondence. All that the church at this stage seemed to be doing was to transform individuals who themselves might create communities of the redeemed within which the standards of the Kingdom would be operative. In the Corinthian church even this ideal seemed a distant one. This does not mean, however, that the church should not be instrumental in inspiring and carrying out the transformation of urban society.

One further incident recorded by Acts as happening to Paul at Corinth was a scene in the court of Gallio, Roman proconsul, brother of Seneca, the famus Stoic philosopher and writer. The charges were brought by Jewish opponents and were strictly religious (Acts 18:12-17).

Gallio, a bit impatient with the Jews anyway, refused to try the case and drove them from the court. In reprisal the group beat up Sosthenes, ruler of the synagogue, and Gallio did nothing to prevent it, illustrating the kind of chicanery and ruthless indifference one sometimes finds in a city.

Paul worked at Corinth a year and a half. After a return to the home base at Antioch, the next big city Paul invaded was Ephesus (Acts 19:1). Ephesus in the province of Asia was even more populous, wealthy, and important than Corinth. From very early times Asia had been dotted with Greek colonies and for many years had been an even more important center of Greek life than Greece itself. The city of Ephesus was originally a colony of Athens, and after the rule of Alexander the Great in the fourth century BC it rose to front rank. By the time of Paul it was at the height of its prosperity. With its location near the entrance to the Maeander valley it stood at the head of the easiest and most traveled route into the interior of Asia Minor. The Romans had made Ephesus a free city, but as capital of the province it was the residence of the proconsul, always a man of highest Roman rank. There was always the closest connection between Rome and Ephesus. Like Corinth it also offered a great challenge to the intrepid apostle to the Gentiles whose cherished goal was Rome itself.

More than any city Paul had yet visited, Ephesus was the home of magic and religion. Round her temples revolved each year a dazzling procession of games and festivals. To order and superintend those in honor of the emperor was one of the chief tasks of the *Asiarchs,* a group consisting of a high priest and his predecessors in office from the chief cities of the province.

Of all the festivals of Ephesus the most spectacular was that of Artemis, or Diana as she was known by the Romans. The temple of Artemis was a structure 425 feet long and 220 feet wide, built over a period of 220 years. The construction was of variegated marble, surrounded with 127 Ionic columns each sixty feet in height and erected by a different monarch to show his devotion to the goddess. A colossal doorway opened upon an interior profusely ornamented with carved ivory and gems, painting and sculpture all lighted by a myriad lamps. In the secret shrine of Artemis was originally the meteorite or sacred stone which fell from heaven, but in Paul's day it had been replaced by a mummy-like figure of the goddess carved from blackened wood or ivory. Coins of the time, some of which Paul himself carried in his purse and used, bear this image of the goddess with her crowned head and many breasts.

We have only a few selected stories of the activities of the church in Ephesus. One happened before Paul arrived; Apollos, a certain Jew of Alexandria and a follower of John the Baptist, came to Ephesus. He is of interest for general New Testament studies and in tracing the spread of the John the Baptist movement and its gradual absorption into Christianity. Apollos' story does not throw specific light on Christianity and the city. It does indirectly say that in the city one meets up with all kinds of sectarian groups, and in the crosscurrents of urban life some strange things can happen. The first story (Acts 19:1-9) told of Paul himself in Ephesus describes a group of Johnites. This time interest centers in their receiving the baptism of the Holy Spirit and the consequent gift of ecstatic speaking as did the first group on Pentecost, the first Samaritans, and the first Gentiles to receive the gospel. Moreover there were exactly twelve, a nice apostolic number, of the John the Baptist people turning to Christianity.

Paul's approach in Ephesus was like that in other cities where there was a synagogue: begin there first, and then when thrown out start among the Greeks and the Romans.

At Ephesus Paul lasted three months in the synagogue, a better record than in most places we know of. Withdrawing and taking his converts with him he found a lecture hall which he could use, one belonging to Tyrannus and probably designed for philosophic instruction. A gloss on some rather ancient manuscripts says that he used the hall from eleven in the morning until four in the afternoon, roughly the period when shops of the city would be closed for midday siesta and he would be able to gather a crowd. He probably did his own manual labor to support himself early in the morning and after four in the afternoon. Here again the atmosphere was specifically that of a Graeco-Roman city where interest in public declamations would be high, a large hall would be available, and scores of daily workers would be resting through the middle of the day and thus free to listen to the public discussions of the gospel. Such an arrangement worked, Luke wrote, for two whole years; and the news of the gospel reached far and wide (Acts 19:8-10).

The two stories which best illustrate the impact of the Christian faith upon Greek city life are the next two (Acts 19:11ff). We now look at some of their important points.

The first incident had to do with the conflict between the true works of God's Spirit in his church and apostles and the works of sorcerers and magicians. As in the early days in Jerusalem, in Ephesus the power of the gospel was so great that God worked many miracles of healing and exorcism, even through the medium of handkerchiefs and aprons. But some traveling exorcists came through and tried to control and make use of the name of Jesus for their own ends. The story is told with no little humor. Seven men claiming to be sons of a high priest tackled one demon under false auspices. What happened to them? The man with a demon leaped upon them, whipped every one of them, and sent them out of their minds and their clothes. This put the fear of God on all the inhabitants of the city. Many who already had become Christian believers, secretly possessing books of magic, came confessing and piling up their books to be burned. (Ephesian books of magic were famous throughout the Empire.) Something over five thousand dollars worth were publicly destroyed. The gospel even affected the reading habits of a city.

The other story, rather long and delightfully told, concerns the economic impact of the gospel on the city. We have already noted the prominence of the temple of Artemis in Ephesus. City pride and patriotic devotion centered in it. A lucrative trade had grown up around the construction of small models of the temple and magic-working images of Artemis for local as well as tourist consumption. The church with its condemnation of idolatry had such an impact upon the city, however, that business had fallen off. Demetrius, president of the guild, was convinced that the situation was critical. With engaging candor Demetrius described first the threat to their business and wealth and then the alarming, but obviously secondary consideration, that the great goddess Artemis might lose out and even be deposed from her supremacy — she who was worshiped not only in all Asia but in the whole world.

For the double threat of losing their business and the reputation of their city and goddess, a convenient scapegoat was discovered in the Christians. The throaty chant began to go up, "Great is Artemis of the Ephesians." From the silversmiths the cry passed to other inhabitants. Soon the whole city was chanting it. Those caught in the maelstrom of mass hypnotism shouted it without the slightest idea of why they did so. Ringleaders found two of the Christians, Gaius and Aristarchus, and dragged them to the amphitheater. A Jew named Alexander attempted to speak, but he further inflamed the crowd which for two hours shouted and milled about in the huge arena. Finally the town clerk succeeded in quieting the mob with the laconic observation that since everyone knew that the city of Ephesus was the keeper of the great Artemis there was no need to shout so loudly about it. The courts were open, if there were charges to be made. Let everything be done peacefully and in good order.

Here again we see characteristics of city life in which the church plays a part: vested interests, the interlocking economic and civic forces, the possibilities of mass demonstrations and mob violence, and the way in which the insistent preaching and witnessing of Christians can affect a questionable business enterprise.

Looking back now over our two Greek cities, Corinth and Ephesus, we might observe in conclusion that urban life, by its concentration of people and the consequent brokenness of community poses some very real problems for Christianity. Among those examined in this chapter are: (1) the entrenchment of various kinds of evils in such concentration that they are not easily rooted out and no one can live in total isolation from them; (2) the suspicion and distrust born of lack of community and communication among city people, infecting even Christianity itself; (3) the close tie-in of vested interests with politics; and (4) the possibility of mass hysteria and mob violence as threats to peace and order.

On the other hand, the city offers some decided advantages for the propagation of Christianity. (1) The very concentration of people means that a greater number can be reached; (2) the superior facilities of the city allow for greater use of mass media of communication (for example, in Ephesus, the Hall of Tyrannus, and today the media of press, radio, and television); and (3) in spite of the tangled nature of urban life, the church can make its impact felt and help change the course of society. We may note further that both Corinth and Ephesus became centers from which Christianity radiated out to other areas. The Aegean port of Corinth, Cenchreae, soon had a church (Rom. 16:1). Out from Ephesus several flourishing congregations were begun. Later Paul had personal converts a hundred miles east of Ephesus in a little cluster of churches in the Lycus valley: Laodicea, Colossae and Hierapolis, where he himself had never personally worked (Col. 4:13-16. Cf. Col. 2:1).

Our cities today, though they face great problems of crime, housing, politics, and economic justice are also at the same time great centers of religion and culture, training centers for Christian leadership, and proving grounds for the work of the church.

10

The Younger and the Older Churches

WE HAVE LOOKED at the expansion of the Christian church over considerable areas of the Roman Empire and have seen its impact upon both Roman and Greek cultures, noting also the particular struggle which it had in large cities. It is time now to pause and consider one interesting phase of this extension of the church scarcely mentioned in the Book of Acts, but one so important and well documented in Paul's letters that it seems right to devote a chapter to it. This is the plan which Paul developed for taking up an offering among his mission churches for the benefit of the mother church in Jerusalem. The detail in the thinking and planning which Paul put into this project enables us to study it at close range as a thrilling chapter in the long history of relations between the younger and the older churches.

For the background of this project, we must go back to the early Jerusalem church and its recurrent problem with food shortage due to famines in Judea and perhaps also to their form of communal living which depleted assets without increasing production. As early as the eleventh chapter of Acts we have mention of a trip which Barnabas and Saul made to Jerusalem with relief goods from the new interracial fellowship at Antioch. Then in Galatians 2:10 (in Paul's concluding statement regarding his consultation in Jerusalem which we tentatively identified with the Council of Jerusalem of Acts 15) there is the request of the Jerusalem church that in his work among the Gentiles he remember the poor. This perhaps meant the poor in other parts of the Christian world, principally Judea. Paul said he was "very eager to do this."

Whether Paul was able to fulfill this request at an earlier date, we do not know. But before his final trip to Jerusalem, about AD 58, we discover him setting the forces in motion for a big offering among his Gentile churches.

Our first reference to the plan comes in the closing paragraphs of First Corinthians (16:1-4). There we learn that already the campaign had begun among the Galatian churches. In a later letter to Corinth Paul used the example of the Macedonian churches to spur the Corinthians along. In the travel plans outlined in Acts 20 there were Asians among Paul's companions. Putting all this evidence together we are justified in concluding that this project included in its scope all of Paul's churches west of Tarsus, or we might say, his entire Gentile mission field up to that time.

We note also from the references in First Corinthians 16 that in the earlier stages of the project Paul was contemplating sending designated representatives from each congregation with the money, while he, apparently, went on with his mission work to the west. As time wore on, however, it became more and more important for Paul to go in person with the deputies from the churches, which he eventually did at great personal risk to himself.

Thus, growing out of the economic need of the churches in Judea, the plan finally expanded to embrace a large number of churches spread over a major portion of Asia Minor and Greece. This project became a kind of second great plan for Paul. His master plan for many years had been to move in a generally westerly direction from Antioch on to Rome and then to Spain in a great sweep across the northern part of the Mediterranean basin. Now this great second plan emerged as an intervening project, one that did not rival but did, for a few years at least, delay his master plan of evangelizing ever onward to the west.

We gather one more hint as to procedure from the passage in First Corinthians 16. This hint is the advice Paul gave the Corinthian church, and one would judge this would be standard procedure everywhere. The money was to be raised over a period of time by putting something aside each Sunday and storing it up. In this way there need not be any crash program or giving under pressure, but regular, systematic planning for this grandly conceived benevolence. Furthermore, the investment by each congregation and the total eventual gift would be larger if thus accumulated over a long period of time.

Our closest and most highly focused picture of the project (presenting much of the thinking that Paul put into it and the appeals he may have used in each church) comes in Second Corinthians, chapters 8 and 9. Here are, by our modern division of the text, thirty-nine verses of solid stewardship, the longest section by far on this subject in the whole New Testament. Here too we are taken behind the scenes into the very fabric of theological meaning of this project. Let us note some of these strands of thought, concentrating especially on those aspects of it which relate the younger to the older churches.

The first thing Paul stressed was sacrificial giving,

spontaneous generosity even in the midst of poverty (2 Cor. 8:1-6). He cited the Macedonian churches as examples to be emulated by the Corinthian church. In a grand mixture of phrases Paul said, "In a severe test of affliction, their abundance of joy and their extreme poverty have overflowed in a wealth of liberality on their part." So enthusiastic were the Macedonian Christians that they not only gave according to their means, a standard he had urged upon the Corinthians in his earlier letter, but far beyond their means. This they did of their own free will, actually begging Paul for the privilege of taking part in this project. One may wonder in a statement like this just where the actual achievement of the Macedonian churches left off and Paul's enthusiasm for the project took over, but together they present an appealing challenge to the Corinthians. Then Paul put to positive work some of the pride and pretension characteristic of the Corinthian Greek mind. He said (2 Cor. 8:7), "Now as you excel in everything — in faith, in utterance, in knowledge, in all earnestness, and in your love for us — see that you excel in this gracious work also."

The example of the Macedonians was not sufficient, however. There was a deeper reason for sharing in this project of giving — the supreme gift of Jesus Christ himself. His grace was such that "though he was rich, yet for your sakes he became poor, so that by his poverty you might become rich" (2 Cor. 8:9). Paul lifted up not only the example of Christ but also the redemptive act of God in Christ as he had preached it so often to each of his churches. Christ, existing in the riches of heavenly glory with his father, had emptied himself in the supreme act of giving in the incarnation, had become the poorest of men, going to a death of utter sacrifice for their sakes. Now they, in grateful acceptance of this gift of salvation, should participate, with the same spirit, in sacrificial giving to others.

Rather abruptly Paul made another type of appeal — that the Corinthians complete what they had begun a year before to do and to enjoy doing, namely the contribution for the saints (2 Cor. 8:10). One might surmise that there had been some lapse in their weekly contributions, especially during a crisis within the life of the church. The earlier spirit of interest is to be revived and they are to have a sense of accomplishment in bringing to a conclusion what they had begun.

Lest the Corinthians feel sorry for themselves or compare themselves with others, Paul made it clear that their gift does not mean that others will have it easy and they will be burdened. Rather there should be a grand and gracious equalizing. The prosperous seaport city of Corinth had enjoyed a level of wealth and comfort not to be found in Jerusalem. The gift was a means by which "your abundance at the present time should supply their want" he told them and then, as he so often did, he balanced this statement with one indicating a higher level of mutuality, "so that their abundance [of spiritual blessings, no doubt] may supply your want [in these areas], that there might be equality." We are dealing here, he said, not with cold economics but with the creative sharing power of God demonstrated in the giving of the manna in the wilderness when "he who gathered much had nothing over, and he who gathered little had no lack" (Ex. 16:18). This spiritual sharing is one of the really exciting aspects of this whole project, and we shall have occasion to come back to it a bit later.

An important dimension in this grand second plan of Paul was the personal one, both in the raising of the money and in its delivery to Jerusalem. Titus, who had worked with this church earlier in the project, before the crisis had arisen, was asked to carry through with it. This man, curiously enough never mentioned in the whole Book of Acts, was one of Paul's most trusted deputies, Paul's own "partner and fellow worker" as he described him (2 Cor. 8:23). The important thing to note here is that this project was no better than the integrity of the men involved in it. This fact is illustrated by the mention of another man, not by name but simply as "the brother who is famous among all the churches for his preaching of the gospel" and later as "our brother whom we have often tested and found earnest in many matters." These two men were to go among the Corinthians, help them raise and gather together their relief funds, perhaps even to serve as bearers of the gifts to Jerusalem. It is interesting to note the great care with which Paul pointed out the reliability of these men, and the genuine trust that the churches had in them. To raise this amount of money for benevolence and entrust it to the safekeeping of a few men was quite a new thing in the experience of these Corinthians. Paul had earlier been falsely accused of trafficking in the gospel, playing on the sympathies of people for gain and absconding with nice sums of money (1 Thess. 2:5), a practice all too common in the ancient world. Great acts of charity require great integrity of character and Paul went out of his way to give the credentials of the two men responsible for this important task. Representatives of any Christian group need to have the backing and trust of the people they represent.

There was another way in which personalities played an important part in this grand scheme and meant so much in the relation of the younger to the older churches. The really dramatic genius of the plan shows itself. For years there had been a suspicion on the part of the older, more conservative churches that maybe these converts of Paul straight from paganism were not quite one hundred percent Christians. How could they be? Were they not fresh from the idolatry and immorality of the pagan cults? What right had they, as latecomers in the Christian faith, to all the blessings which God through centuries of time had been channeling through Judaism? The presence of good, clean-cut Gentile Christians would not only shut the mouth of any critics but would help provide the proof needed that the Gentile mission was truly ordained of God and productive of true Christian results. Think of the thrill today to the church in America when strong, up-standing converts with a zeal and devotion which puts our own to shame come to us from India, Africa, and the Far East to let us know that the mission to the nations is indeed the work of God. It is with new interest that we read of Sopater of Beroea, Aristarchus and Secundus of Thessalonica, Gaius of Derbe, Timothy of Lystra, and Tychicus and Trophimus from the province of Asia (Acts 20:1-5). These are some of the picked deputies chosen to bear both the gifts and the warm handclasp of Christian fellowship as a gesture of appreciation from the younger churches to the mother church in Jerusalem. Think of the dramatic possibilities as Paul, himself the epitome of the worldwide mission enterprise, came at great personal risk to himself, and around him a group of dedicated, thankful Christians of various national and cultural backgrounds, and in person they laid at the feet of the Jerusalem church a handsome gift of love and shared life!

Beyond these persons, however, and giving meaning to them and to the whole inspired project, was the work of God who used this demonstration of love and gratitude to bring new dimensions of blessing to his church. Going on into the ninth chapter of Second Corinthians we discover some further aspects of this growing blessing.

First is the law of sowing and reaping applied to the whole realm of generosity. "He who sows sparingly will also reap sparingly, and he who sows bountifully will also reap bountifully." A word from Jesus has it "Give and it will be given to you; good measure, pressed down, shaken together, running over, will be put into your lap. For the measure you give will be the measure you get back" (Luke 6:38). Now this is not mechanical or automatic. The one who attempts to manipulate or control it in any way falls into the error of Ananias and Sapphira, of Simon Magus and the seven sons of Sceva. How then does it work? It works by the creative power of God the great Giver.

People are to sow as God sows love and goodness, with joyful free will. "Each one must do as he has made up his mind," said Paul, "not reluctantly or under compulsion; God loves a cheerful giver." Then he spoke again of the reward. This is always dangerous in a way. For people by nature want to control things or dictate to God the timing and terms of results. What Paul said is that "God is able to provide you with every blessing in abundance so that you may always have enough of everything" (2 Cor. 9:8). But beware, God gives this by his grace, not on our demand. Furthermore, "enough of everything" is by God's measure of what is enough for us, not the measure of our ever-growing greed and rising wants. Paul believed that if Christians are generous in contributing to the Lord's work, there will be rewards spilling over and returning to the giver sufficient for his needs and enough for him to go on providing "in abundance in every good work."

Now, lest we think that this reward is primarily material, Paul proceeded to point out that the true increase is an increase in righteousness and the enrichment is to the whole man, "in every way" so as to "produce thanksgiving to God." All of this he was saying to the comparatively new converts at Corinth, members of one of the "younger churches" with respect to their love offering for the older churches. If he had been writing to the older Christians he would have written much the same thing. The best way for the younger churches to relate themselves to the older ones is in the ministry of gracious and generous giving. As he explained (2 Cor. 9:12), the service filled basic human need and produced grateful thanks to God, that is, in worship and spiritual growth. Paul saw here a real opportunity for his younger churches to grow in their appreciation of the gospel which they had received free of charge because others before them had cared enough.

The gospel is based on grace and giving from beginning to end. In the creation God gave of himself. In sending his Son into the world he gave. God in Christ also gave constantly of himself in the ministry of compassionate service, and then gave himself completely and supremely on the cross. The resurrection was likewise a great act of giving on God's part, pouring forth divine power in triumph. Similarly the creation of the church through the ministry of the risen Lord and the outpoured Spirit at Pentecost were continued acts of giving. The mission to the nations required the constant giving on the part of God in Christ, responded to by the self-giving of countless Spirit-filled witnesses and missionaries.

So Paul asked the younger churches to acknowledge the gospel of Christ, this gospel of giving, by participating in it. The particular project at the moment was a thank offering to those who had made possible the sending of the gospel to them. Nor was this the whole picture. The older church, in spite of some provincialism at times, "really longs for and prays for you," Paul wrote, "because of the surpassing grace of God at work in you." The total vision of this working of God's generous grace in both the older and the younger churches was so tremendous that in conclusion Paul broke forth in gratitude to Almighty God for beginning this work in Christ: "Thanks be to God for his inexpressible gift!"

The Corinthians and others responded to Paul's appeal and in the course of time the contributions from the various congregations were gathered. The representatives made ready for the long journey to Jerusalem. During the last few weeks before sailing Paul dictated his longest and most significant literary work, the powerful Epistle to the Romans, in which he again mentioned this great project (Rom. 15:25-28). Among other things he spoke of the debt which the younger churches owed to the older ones, for they shared in their spiritual blessings and ought to be of service to them in a material way.

Acts tells us of the historic trip to Jerusalem, lists the names of a few of the individuals involved and makes one passing reference (Acts 24:17) to the alms and offerings which Paul brought, but tells us nothing further about it. Surely we can say that, regardless of our ignorance of its immediate results, this grand attempt to awaken both the newer and older churches to their mutual bond of unity in Christ must have made its due contribution to the church of the first century. Perhaps even more significant is the way in which, through the sections of the New Testament (especially 2 Cor. 8 — 9 and Rom. 15) which it inspired, it continues to work for unity and benevolence among all churches of Christ, both older and younger, to this day.

11

The Church as a Legal Revolution

IN THE PREVIOUS CHAPTER we went outside of Acts into significant portions of Paul's letters to the Corinthians and Romans to fill in the story of the offering of the Gentile Christians for the mother church in Jerusalem. Now we want to pick up the thread of the story in Acts again, with particular emphasis upon the various court appearances, trials, and defenses which Paul made as recorded from Acts 21 through 26.

The casual reader of Acts in our day may pause and wonder what is the meaning of this rather bewildering series of arrests, trials, and acquittals of Paul through this section of the book, all told with great detail and apparently very important to the author and the intended ancient reader. What is it all about? Is it important to go through all this? If so, what does it contribute to our understanding of the nature of the early church?

To get underneath this section of Acts we need to

take a brief look at the whole book, in fact at the two-volume work Luke-Acts, and note something that scholars have been telling us for some time. One of the primary reasons, if not the basic reason, for the writing of the two books is to demonstrate that Christianity is no novel cult, newly and illicitly forcing itself upon the Roman Empire, but that, quite the contrary, it is the divinely directed outgrowth of Judaism, a very ancient and venerated religion. Furthermore, time and time again, when the proponents of Christianity were opposed and brought before the courts, Roman law upheld them. They were not lawbreakers.

Once this intention of the writer is pointed out to us, his especially detailed series of accounts of court trials and public defenses of the gospel begins to make sense. Over and over again the author showed that, subjected to whatever kind of examination the opponents and critics of the faith wished to bring against it, Christianity came out cleared from all suspicion of illegality or illegitimacy.

There is another feature of the combined work, Luke-Acts, which needs to be set alongside the "legality" of the gospel and that is the fact that Christianity is a revolutionary faith. It is new wine poured into old wineskins. Individuals and groups seized by it are never the same again. Told three times over through the book of Acts in as widely separated chapters as the ninth, the twenty-second, and the twenty-sixth, is the exciting story of the conversion of Saul-Paul. God worked a revolution in the life of a fiery persecutor of the faith to transform him into an equally zealous preacher of the gospel he once tried to destroy. So revolutionary is this faith that its opponents are quoted as testifying that the Christian missionaries "have turned the world upside down" (Acts 17:6). These hostile witnesses were right about the revolutionary power of the gospel. They were wrong, however, about the direction of the turning. The world was already upside down. Christians were turning it right side up!

We therefore have a paradox: the church is legal in every way, legitimate and divinely ordained, yet it is profoundly revolutionary, transforming all who embrace it, or are embraced by it. It is nonsubversive in the way in which its opponents charged it being, but it was very subversive of the evil which ever lurked in the intentions of men and nations in their rebellion against God.

With this clue in mind let us first note that all through Luke-Acts there are crisis situations calling forth this paradox we are calling the "legal revolution." In what is regarded as the frontispiece of Luke, the story of the rejection at Nazareth in the fourth chapter, Jesus was opposed by his townsmen for his proclaiming the gospel in Old Testament language as good news for the poor, release of captives, recovering of sight for the blind, setting at liberty the oppressed, and announcing the year of the Lord's favor. This thoroughly scriptural platform was certainly "legal" and yet revolutionary. Something of its upsetting aspect became apparent as Jesus went on to quote two stories from Scripture in which Gentiles were blessed by God in preference to members of the chosen people (Luke 4:25-27). As a result, the people of Nazareth turned into an angry mob, indicting him not by legal means but by mob action and attempting to do away with him completely.

Again at the trial of Jesus in Jerusalem the same complex of forces was at work. The so-called trial of Stephen (Acts 7) was really mob action in violation of legal procedure. The opponents of the faith got their man but violated both their own laws and the conscience of mankind in doing so.

And so it is throughout all the early chapters of Acts, the hearings of Peter and John before the Sanhedrin out of which came the thoroughly incontrovertible position that "we ought to obey God rather than man" and in the various instances in his earlier missionary travels in which

Paul was attacked and brought before the law: at Philippi, Thessalonica, Corinth, and Ephesus. Each of these incidents contained a little different slant and charge, but each contained an acquittal of the apostles of the faith before the conscience of the Graeco-Roman world, the world of the early reader of the book.

As we turn now in the latter chapters of Acts to the various defenses of the gospel which Paul made, we find an interesting series of illustrations of this twin truth of the "legal revolution." The crowd was stirred up against Paul over a supposed appearance of his in the temple with a Gentile (Acts 21:27ff). They rushed upon Paul in their fury and almost killed him before the Roman soldiers rescued him. At once we see how illegal was this attack upon Paul. First, the charge was but a supposition and not grounded in fact; but even if true, what was the crime in the sight of God of bringing a Gentile into the temple of the Creator of the world? The revolutionary character of the Christian faith is seen in the fact that the time had come for all nationalities and races of men to be allowed equal access to the courts of God.

A Roman officer confused Paul with the Egyptian who had been stirring up political rebellion (Acts 21:37ff). Not only did Paul prove his innocence of this charge — again, he was legal, you see — but he went on, speaking in good Greek, to show his Jewish background and his Roman citizenship — a triple-threat man at home in three cultures.

Again, in Paul's defense on the stairway (Acts 22), the two-edged aspect of Christianity was shown. The Christian gospel is highly revolutionary in that it took a zealous persecutor of the church and transformed him into an intrepid preacher of the faith, himself persecuted. At every step he was led by the God of their fathers to do what he did: the voice and great light on the road to Damascus, Ananias of Damascus, devotion to the law, his commission by God himself to be a witness to all nations, and the heavenly vision which has always marked the true servant of God.

Here as in several other defenses in and around Jerusalem the solid connection between Christianity and Judaism was stressed. Yet when Paul went on to say that he was a missionary to the Gentiles, the very mention of the word sent the people into such a rage that they cried out, waved their garments in the air, and tried to kill him. Examination by the Roman soldiers who had tied him and were about to scourge him revealed that he was a Roman citizen by birth. Since it was a crime punishable by death to scourge a Roman citizen (especially as they were going to do it, without so much as a trial), Paul's legal rights were brought into dramatic focus.

Paul's next hearing was before the high court, the Sanhedrin. There, for simply contending that he had lived before God in all good conscience up to that day, he was ordered to be slapped on the mouth, a command which any careful reader will recognize was totally unworthy both of the office of the high priest and of the august court of the Holy God. Paul lashed back in understandable anger and prophetic judgment upon the high priest for this act, only to be reminded that this was God's high priest. His reply is an enigma, "I did not know, brethren, that he was the high priest; for it is written, 'you shall not speak evil of a ruler of your people' " (Acts 23:5). Did Paul, perhaps because of bad eyesight, actually fail to recognize the high priest? Or is this a bit of biting sarcasm, as much as to say, "Well, I would never have known you were the high priest by the way you acted"? Again Paul maintained legality as he admitted, "You shall not speak evil of a ruler of your people."

Paul's astuteness in dividing the council over the resurrection issue (between Pharisees who believed in bodily resurrection and Sadducees who did not) serves again to show up a superficiality in the opposition which would put on trial this leader of the church. Imagine these dignified and godly jurors whipped up into such a rage that they tore at Paul like animals, until the pagan Roman officer, out of sheer enforcement of good order, rescued Paul from their midst.

The next series of stories contains a high level of human interest also centering on the essential innocence of this controversial and revolutionary man Paul, representative of the "legal revolution" of the early church. Let us follow the story (Acts 23:11-35):

First Paul was assured by divine vision that no matter what happened he would reach Rome to testify. This gave him the confidence to move forward no matter how great the odds against him.

Then a plot was made against his life, a most serious plot of more than forty assassins who bound themselves by oath neither to eat nor sleep until they had killed him. Not only did they make this death pact, but they had a clever ruse for getting Paul delivered into their hands. The high court was to ask for Paul to be brought down to them for further hearing and on the way they would ambush and kill him.

A young nephew of Paul's possibly a teenager or perhaps even younger, with a youngster's knack of overhearing important conversations, picked up information about the plot. He slipped into the guardhouse and told his Uncle Paul. Paul asked the centurion in charge to take the boy to the tribune and to tell his story. The whole murderous scheme was laid before the tribune. The tribune took the word of the young fellow and told him to keep silent as a counter plan began to take shape in his fertile mind. Instead of one helpless man led by a couple of guards, an easy prey for their plans, the forty assassins suddenly had to contend with two hundred infantry, seventy men on horses, and an added two hundred spearmen.

And they were headed not for the court as they expected but for Caesarea, seat of the provincial government.

Not only do stories like this make interesting reading, but more importantly, they underscore the fact that it was not Christianity but its radical opponents who were playing the illegal game and that Christ's representatives, though terribly revolutionary, were the innocent victims of scheming men.

The reader cannot help but smile at the note which Lysias, the Roman tribune, wrote to his superior officer, the governor at Caesarea (Acts 23:26-30). In it he said that he had rescued Paul because he learned he was a Roman citizen. Actually he had ordered Paul to be tied up and illegally whipped and was only stopped when Paul himself volunteered the information that he was a Roman citizen and not to be subjected to such illegal treatment. But, though the tribune put himself in a most favorable light, a common human tendency, he did make clear that Paul was about to be killed over matters of theology and not because he was guilty of anything deserving death or imprisonment.

Paul's two years or more around the imperial headquarters at Caesarea, like his protracted imprisonment around Rome later, were trying ones filled with governmental red tape, unexplained delays, and tedious, time-killing tactics. But for our purposes, the important thing to watch is the way in which again and again Paul and his cause, the Christian Church, were tested and acquitted.

The first test was a round with the high priest and other high officials of the Sanhedrin represented by their attorney Tertullus (Acts 24). The point here is the contrast between the extreme charges of the lawyer — that Paul was a pestilent fellow, an agitator and profaner of the temple, one so bad that a simple examination would convince the Roman governor of his guilt — and the true facts. When the examination was held, Paul proceeded to show convincingly that he was not disputing in the temple or anywhere else in the city. His only crime was that he was a Christian, a worshiper of the God of the Fathers, believer in the law and the prophets. All through here the connection is made between the Christian church, through Paul its representative, and Judaism, particularly with the newer Judaism which embraced the concept of the resurrection of the dead, with respect to which he was on trial that day.

The governor, Antonius Felix, himself an ex-slave or freedman now risen to high office, put off a decision in the case until the arrival of Lysias, the tribune. Details of the next hearing, in which Felix and his wife heard Paul speak directly to them, are not given, except that as Paul laid the claims of God squarely before them in terms of justice, self-control, and future judgment, the politically minded Felix squirmed and put him off (Acts 24:24f). The talk around the palace was that the governor was angling for a nice bribe from Paul and so had frequent sessions with him. Instead of the money he wanted, Paul gave him the gospel, and the private duel was ended only by the recall and replacement of Felix by another governor, Porcius Festus. But Felix, still playing both sides of the street, left Paul in prison. The severe testing of the Christian faith was not finished.

The next stage in establishing the legality of Christianity was its removal from the orbit of Palestinian politics to the Roman courts. At the changing of governors, the chief priests and leaders in Jerusalem tried again to get Paul into their hands, planning as before an assassination ambush. Either through ignorance or proper political caution in a new situation, the new governor refused to play into their hands and set the hearing in Caesarea, the seat of the Roman provincial government. When forced to make a decision as to whether or not to return to Jerusalem and be tried, Paul made a formal appeal to appear before Caesar in Rome (Acts 25:11). From our distance we may think that this was a mistake on Paul's part, especially when we realize that Caesar was the notorious Nero, later to achieve ill fame for his persecution of the Christians and the man under whom Paul himself was finally martyred. But from the perspective of Paul and the message of the Book of Acts this was no mistake, nor need one feel regretful later when Paul was told by Agrippa II that he could have been set free had he not appealed to Caesar (Acts 26:32).

First of all, we note that Paul was following the instruction given him in divine vision when the Lord stood by him in the night and said that he must bear witness at Rome (Acts 23:11). Furthermore, we must note that Paul's appeal gave Christianity one of its first opportunities to be heard officially in the court of Caesar and to stand the test of legality before the highest human tribunal in the western world. Surely the author of Acts was thinking of a combination of both these considerations: the divinely directed testing of Christianity before man's highest court, so that the legitimacy of the faith might be shown to all the world, even while it revolutionized men and nations. "You have appealed to Caesar," Festus said, "to Caesar you shall go."

Next entered the drama a colorful figure, Agrippa II, who, at thirty-three had already been serving some twelve years or more around Palestine as king of various outlying territories and general liaison officer between Romans and Jews. A great-grandson of old King Herod, he was brought up in Caesar's court in Rome and combined the shrewdness of high Roman society with a somewhat dilettante interest in things Jewish. He was accompanied by his sister Bernice. Porcius Festus, the Roman governor, welcomed Agrippa's counsel in this troublesome case. For the Book of Acts, Agrippa serves as sort of legal bridge between Roman and Jewish authority.

First the governor explained the case to King Agrippa in terms which Acts has been maintaining throughout, that really the charges against Paul (hence against the whole Christian church) were not of crimes punishable by the court of law, but theological matters such as the resurrection from the dead.

The following day Agrippa and his sister arrived with typical Roman pomp and ceremony as befitted the seat of the imperial government for Palestine (Acts 25:23). At the appropriate time Paul, the prisoner, was ushered in. Again the governor summarized the case, ending with the observation that after finding that Paul had done nothing deserving death, and yet had appealed to Caesar, he, the governor, needed something to write to his emperor about. "It seems to me unreasonable," said he, "in sending a prisoner, not to indicate the charges against him." So the hard-bitten Roman governor was hard put to it to find any real charges to bring against the chief missionary of the Christian church.

This gave Paul an opportunity to retell the ever-dramatic story of his early life and conversion, and the author's third opportuntiy in the book to lay this account before his readers. The special accent in this telling, if there is one, seems to be the age-old gospel of repentance and forgiveness, the relevance of which soon became apparent. Again the point was made that Christianity is the true extension of Judaism from Moses and the prophets as fulfilled in the suffering, death, and resurrection of the Messiah with his gospel for all nations.

The reaction to this defense is interesting. Festus responded with a loud voice declaring Paul insane, the result of his great learning. At least there is nothing criminal about him — he is just crazy. Paul then had an opportunity to point out that this message was not insanity but sober truth. He appealed to King Agrippa for evidence that the historical basis of Christianity was indeed plain historical fact. Then he pressed him yet harder, asking him for a confession of faith. He believed the prophets, did he not? Sensing the direction the hearing was taking, the king squirmed and exclaimed that Paul was attempting to make a Christian out of him. "Not a bad idea," responded Paul, "I would to God that not only you, but also all who hear me this day might become such as I am." Then he happened to look down and see his handcuffs, and swiftly added, "Except for these chains."

Although the hope of converting a hard-bitten Roman governor and a dissolute descendant of Herod might seem so remote as to be absurd, it was not farfetched. It is the contention of Acts that those in high office need the gospel just as much, if not more, than do others. Furthermore, Paul himself had already had considerable success with men like Sergius Paul and was still later to convert members of Caesar's praetorian guard (Phil. 1:13; 4:22). In fact, the time was not too distant that not only Roman governors and puppet kings were to become Christian but Roman emperors and all their subjects were to own the name of Christ.

The common judgment of Festus and Agrippa was sound: "This man is doing nothing to deserve death or imprisonment" — a familiar theme by this time. "In fact," added Agrippa, "he could have been set free if he had not appealed to Caesar."

The meaning of all this for the church as a legal revolution is clear and revealing. The church is legal, in fact, so innocent of the charge of political subversion that the highest authorities of Palestine, represented by both local and imperial authorities, gave it a clean bill of health, proclaiming it legally free. And yet, because it is a world-wide faith, it was not free, but must go bound to Rome until man himself is set free from the sin which holds him in bondage.

12

The Church and Rome

IN THE PREVIOUS CHAPTER we saw that as a result of divine vision and the direction in which his court trials led him, Paul was headed for Rome. "You have appealed to Caesar; to Caesar you shall go," said the procurator Festus.

We pick up our story in Acts 27:1. Paul was delivered in chains to a centurion named Julius to be conducted by him to Rome as Caesar Nero's personal prisoner. In the party were also two Christian companions, Aristarchus of Thessalonica and Luke, the physician and author of Acts. There are many interesting features of their travel arrangements about which we are ignorant, but there is no question as to the major direction of movement and the intent of Acts to bring us to its conclusion in Rome. The story is told (Acts 27 and 28) with the precision of a ship's log and the color of an adventure story. For our purposes in seeking to understand the early church we shall take care to look at the account from the perspective, not of Paul the individual, but of Paul as representative of the vital Christian movement which had been, for some years now, in the process of "going to Rome."

For the present-day reader there may seem to be a bewildering array of names and places in Acts 27 and 28 which may not mean too much. They may, in fact, actually impede the flow of the story. But for the ancient reader these place-names were significantly Roman: such details as the ports of call, the kinds and names of ships, and the many colorful aspects of ship handling. Paul was on the Roman trade routes and his experiences, except for his fetters, were those of thousands of other Romans of the times traveling about the empire.

It was already late autumn, nearing the end of the shipping season. The first boat which Paul and his party took was bound for a port up along Asia Minor near Troas and it kept close to the shore. At a port called Myra the centurion found another ship, one of the big imperial grain ships plying from Egypt to Rome trying to make one last trip before the winter storms cut off all travel. But the winds were against them and one delay after another impeded their journey.

On several occasions during the voyage Paul offered advice or leadership. He was concerned about the saving of human lives. But his suggestion that to continue would cost cargo and lives was outvoted by his centurion and the vested interests on board who were intent on getting the grain on toward Rome as fast as possible, regardless of the human risk. Paul was demonstrating the prophetic function of the church and insisted on the priority of human welfare even against materialistic interests.

The next exciting adventure was a story (Acts 27:13-44) told by Luke with great perception and detail. Any Graeco-Roman reader who had ever matched wits and skill with the mighty Mediterranean in a sailing vessel would follow this story with real interest: the blast of the tempestuous northeaster, the storm-tossed sea, long days and nights without sight of sun or stars, forced fasting from anxiety. Paul came forward again as a prophet, this time to predict the saving of all lives on board despite a coming shipwreck. So sure was Paul that he would stand before Caesar in Rome that he assured even the outright pagans that his God would save all lives.

After being driven by the storm for two whole weeks, the sailors were at the breaking point and about to abandon ship, leaving everyone else to certain death at sea. Again Paul, spokesman for Christian fairness and concern, stepped into the crisis, and this time convinced Julius, his private centurion, and the soldiers on board that all would be lost unless they thwarted the selfish plans of the sailors.

The next morning Paul performed another churchly function of great significance. Noting the mounting tension and the weakening of morale from lack of food, Paul, in a manner reminiscent of the risen Lord who made himself known in the breaking of the bread, took bread, gave thanks, broke it, and began to eat. This sacramental and eminently practical act broke the tension, and everyone, Christian and pagan alike, took food. Not only was the whole group strengthened, but the people were now sensible enough to lighten the cargo and make more possible the saving of human lives.

Another crisis arose as the ship ran upon a shoal (Acts 27:41) and began to break up in the surf. The soldiers planned to kill all the prisoners lest they escape. This, of course, would have meant the end of Paul and perhaps of his companions, Luke and Aristarchus. The centurion Julius intervened to save the day, though earlier he had preferred to listen to the ship's captain and owner rather than to Paul. Thus Paul's prediction came true as all 276 of the ship's personnel were saved on the island of Malta.

The interesting adventure with the snake on Malta

(Acts 28:1-6) is told from a Roman perspective with Paul again emerging as the hero. Like the Greeks before them, Romans called all out-of-the-way and primitive peoples "barbarians" and attributed to them all sorts of superstitious beliefs. One minute the Maltese suspected Paul of being the vilest of criminals and a bit later hailed him as a god, the direct reverse of the emotional swing of the fickle inhabitants of Lystra (Acts 14:8-20). A royal reception by Publius, Roman ruler of the island, the miraculous cure of Publius' father, and then widespread healings helped fill up the three-month winter sojourn on Malta.

As spring opened up the 276 miscellaneous passengers, sailors, soldiers, merchants and prisoners, a group who had gone through near tragedy and miraculous new life together, found another Egyptian grain ship and made a quick trip to the Italian port of Puteoli where the imperial fleet customarily docked.

Once arrived in Italy, Paul was among Christians. He spent seven days at Puteoli, where his guard Julius graciously permitted him to enjoy the fellowship of the church. News of Paul's arrival sped on to Rome and Roman Christians met him out along the Appian Way and escorted him into the city. Twice (Acts 28:14b and 16a) Luke speaks of coming to Rome with a sigh of relief and a cry of triumphant fulfillment as the story of Acts draws swiftly to its close.

We leave the fast-moving story of Acts with one final episode which echoes an earlier emphasis. Paul called together the Roman leaders of the Jews, explained his case, found them not particularly prejudiced against him but skeptical of the Christian movement. On an appointed day he expounded the gospel from morning till evening. The result was the usual one among Jews. Some were convinced and became believers; others, probably the majority, did not believe, and a controversy arose. As the group broke up, Paul quoted against them a strong section from Isaiah 6 about hardness of heart and disbelief and declared, what is also a central theme of Acts, "Let it be known then that this salvation of God has been sent to the Gentiles; they will listen" (Acts 28:28).

The Book of Acts closes with this and a brief summary of the next two years of Paul's life in Rome. Awaiting trial, he continued what he had been doing all along: "preaching the kingdom of God and teaching about the Lord Jesus Christ quite openly and unhindered."

And so Paul came to Rome, and Luke closed his two-volume work, Luke-Acts. But by this time Christianity had already been in Rome for many years. Just when it reached the imperial city and who carried it, we have no way of knowing. Some think that possibly as early as AD 29, pilgrims from Rome attending the feast of Pentecost carried the new gospel back to the center of the Empire. Surely sometime between that date and the expulsion of the Jews under the Emperor Claudius in AD 49, Christians had reached the city and Christian groups had formed. It is probable that Priscilla and Aquila were already Christians when they came from Rome and joined Paul at Corinth (Acts 18:2). Certainly by AD 58, some three years before Paul's arrival in Rome, there was a substantial church in Rome, as we learn from Paul's well-known Epistle to the Romans. Furthermore, every evidence would support the view that it was begun by unknown and unsung Christians, to whom Paul, who was very careful not to trespass on the mission field of other apostles, could write a letter so full of doctrine and advice as Romans is.

For the remainder of this story of the church and Rome, we must go beyond Acts and note first the way in which Rome, from this time forward, became a kind of literary center for the Christian movement. Paul himself contributed greatly to this with his prison epistles. While there have been attempts to locate the writing of some of his prison epistles in other cities, Caesarea, for example, or Ephesus, the view still prevails that the majority of Paul's prison epistles were written from the capital of the Empire.

One pair of letters which Paul wrote while in prison, and in our judgment from Rome, revolved around the human interest story of the runaway slave Onesimus. In the letter to Philemon, Paul attempted to reconcile the converted slave, who by Roman law could be punished by death, with his Christian master. The other letter is Colossians, sent at the same time to the church where Philemon and Onesimus lived.

Another letter, in all likelihood a later and expanded edition of Colossians, may be traced to Paul's time in Rome (or, as some think, to a later writer modeling a letter after Colossians and other of Paul's writings). This letter is Ephesians, one of the strongest expressions in the New Testament of the doctrine of the church as the church universal, the body of Christ and heir of the eternal promises of God.

Still another letter may be regarded as arising out of Paul's Roman experience and that is Philippians. Paul was facing either release from prison or death. He wrote to express thanks for gifts his old church at Philippi had sent and to tell how the gospel had been spreading even among the praetorian guard who held him prisoner.

These letters of Paul from Rome tell us that not only did he continue his literary activity while in prison, but out of that Roman prison came some of the ripened fruitage of his years of work. Generally speaking, in the prison epistles we find the reflective, judicious, and mellow Paul, his active journeys over and his Christian attitudes strengthened and enriched.

Other important books of the New Testament can, with more or less certainty, be traced to Roman origin.

The earliest of our Gospels, the Gospel of Mark, is

rather generally believed to have been written in Rome, probably primarily for the benefit of the Roman church. Its emphasis upon a Christ of authority who knowingly took up the cross and prepared his disciples to accept the way of the cross as witnesses unto the uttermost — all this fits the church at Rome in the sixties, under the persecution of the Emperor Nero.

First Peter likewise is regarded as emanating from Rome, a preparation of Christians for the fiery trials that were to come upon them. Scholars differ as to whether the letter referred to the Rome of Nero's time or later in the nineties under the Emperor Domitian. In either case, it does reflect the martyr church at Rome.

And so we might go on and mention other writings of our New Testament composed in Rome or with the Roman church in mind. But these two tell us something of the character of this church, and witness to its rising importance as the church in the capital of the Empire.

A most valuable source of information about the Roman church at the end of the first century (late nineties or early one hundreds) is the writing called First Clement, not found in our New Testament but included in what we usually call the "Apostolic Fathers." This letter, from a certain Clement, Bishop of Rome, to the Christians at Corinth rebukes them for a revolt movement among them which led to their deposing the bishops and deacons. The Roman church, through its spokesman Clement, put in writing what was becoming its prevailing view of the divinely appointed leadership of the church. God had sent Christ, they said, and Christ had sent the apostles, and these, on their missionary journeys had installed bishops and deacons, as explicitly prophesied in Isaiah 60:17. Therefore bishops and deacons who exercise their office blamelessly cannot be deposed on any account.

Rome was the place of martyrdom of Peter and Paul, the two great apostles celebrated in the Book of Acts.

This in itself, as years and centuries passed, tended to give this city a hallowed place in Christian history.

A writing of the New Testament, not produced in Rome, but having a great deal to do with that city and registering a sharp condemnation of the Roman Empire and of the city of Rome is the Book of Revelation, the last one listed in our New Testament canon. Written to help Christians prepare for a fight to the death against the pagan worship of the emperor this writing predicted God's judgment upon Rome and the destruction of the city, contemptuously called Babylon the Great. In this book we see brought out the other side of the coin of greatness — great corruption and great destruction. While Christians in Rome enjoyed something of the prestige of that city, still they found it difficult to disentangle themselves from the evil of the city as represented in its idolatry, immorality, and emperor worship.

The Roman church went on to become both spiritually and politically powerful, its bishops more and more prominent in the total life of the western church. Eastern churches centered in the Greek cities were not always happy with this domination, but the trend continued. Likewise churches in other parts of the Empire, like the Assyrian church to the east and the Coptic church in Egypt, went their own ways.

While Christianity was still a persecuted minority, the connection between the church and the state was one of rather healthy tension which kept the church free of some of the power politics which later invaded it. But when, two and a half centuries after the story of Acts, there arose a Roman emperor who became Christian and who made all his subjects Christian, at one stroke as it were, then two things happened which affected the course of Christianity for centuries afterward.

The general level of genuine Christianity was greatly adulterated by the wholesale taking into the church of large numbers of people who were Christians only in name. The other thing that happened was the uniting of ecclesiastical and political power which led to many abuses down through the medieval period; a situation which has only in part been corrected on American soil by the separation of church and state.

In attempting to evaluate the going of the church to Rome, we discover that we have no simple case. On the good side were the undoubted advantages of having a strong Christian group at the center of the Empire, resulting in such achievements as the publication and distribution of Christian literature, the organizing and structuring of church life, and the preserving of mainstream Christianity against various distortions of it. Furthermore, one can say that historically it was inevitable that Christianity go to Rome. Not only did all roads lead there, but Christianity belonged there where so many of the policy decisions of the civilized world were made.

On the negative side of the ledger, however, one would note that even in the first century the Roman church, by virtue of its position, soon assumed a considerable measure of prestige and authority. When the church finally did triumph and became the religion of the emperor and of his subjects, there was a widespread mixing of Christianity with paganism and an allying of the church with political power, a situation which later made necessary the Protestant Reformation and successive reform movements.

In conclusion, we might observe that both the positive and negative features of "going to Rome" should convince us that this historical fact has been of utmost importance to the whole story of the Christian church, and worthy of our serious study.

13

The Church and Succeeding Generations

IT IS FITTING NOW to draw this brief study of the early church to a close with a sketch drawn from a group of New Testament writings which reflect a period after the story told in Acts. These writing include what we call the General Epistles and Revelation, produced after the writings of Paul. Generalizations are often dangerous, even those made about "general epistles," but it will not be out of place to note the ongoing situation of the church in the period following the close of the story of Acts. We shall examine major problems and the contribution which these general writings made to the solution of these problems.

The Book of Acts, as we have seen, describes the earliest Christian church, composed of first-generation Christians, many of them on the frontiers or mission fields of the church. First-generation Christians, with their enthusiasms and problems, are also dealt with in Paul's letters. But when we turn to the so-called General Epistles we begin to see looming up some of the problems which arise as Christianity is passed on to succeeding generations and carried out farther and farther into areas and cultures quite removed from the original birthplace of the faith.

One of the most serious problems to face anyone who is reared from childhood in the faith (that is, a second-, third-, or later-generation Christian) is the loss of the original enthusiasm and fervor which characterizes a sharp and sudden changeover from one way of life to another. One brought into the church as a genuine convert from paganism is usually a Christian with a definite religious experience, and a grateful one at that. He is so impressed by the new life he finds in Christ that right from the start he has an enthusiasm that carries him far in terms of perseverance, the endurance of suffering, and the various levels of witness. But let one grow up from childhood in the faith, breathing it in with the air, absorbing it with his daily food, accepting it as he does the general blessings of society about him, and the cutting edge of Christianity is almost sure to be dulled. To him Christianity is something like general education, public health, or the law of the land. It is the easiest thing in the world for such a person to "take his Christianity for granted," or by a slip of the tongue, even to "take it for granite," a dead weight, something to be borne.

It is helpful to know that there are epistles in the New Testament written precisely to meet such a problem, one which we instinctively know to be our problem today. Let us take a brief look at one or two examples.

One of these is found in the writing called First Peter. Tradition associates this with the Apostle Peter and if that is true it reflects the life of the church sometime during the persecution by Nero in the 60's. Some scholars think it may reflect a period considerably later in the first century. Regardless of date, it does get at this problem of taking one's religion for granted by containing several statements designed to help Christians appreciate what they have. One of these is in 1 Peter 1:10-12 where Christians are made to see that all the light of sacred history was focused upon them. It was not for their own benefit, says the author, that the prophets were speaking but for you Christians, heirs of such treasures that even angels long to look into them. Christians are made to square their shoulders with such bracing talk as this: "You are a chosen race, a royal priesthood, a holy nation, God's own people" — good tonic for all who might be inclined to take their faith for granted.

The whole message is a powerful emphasis upon the superiority of Christ and his gospel to all other forms of religion. Particularly would people tempted to fall back either into the Judaism or paganism out of which they had come be helped to appreciate what they had in Christ. For Christ, as the author marshalled his evidence to prove, is far above the angels, greater than Moses through whom the law was given, and superior to the high priest and the sacrificial system, in fact, One who embodies all that these means of divine grace have to offer and a great deal more.

In Hebrews, the appeal to succeeding generations takes the form of exhortation to Christians to lift their drooping hands and strengthen their weak knees (Heb. 12:12), for later-generation Christians easily grow weary. Furthermore, there are strong challenges to go on to maturity, to leave the elementary doctrines, and to grow up in Christ (Heb. 6:1ff). Christians are not to neglect their meeting together (Heb. 10:25) nor acts of service (Heb. 3:1-3, 16). Along with this is still another type of teaching: a stern warning against backsliding, or returning to former inferior faiths or of slipping off into a deadly secularism (Heb. 10:26-39). If we are honest, we shall see ourselves and our kind of problems reflected here.

In the medieval manuscripts from which the King

James translation was made, Hebrews was ascribed to Paul, but nowhere is his name mentioned in the text. The style and subject matter are so different from his known epistles that the judgment of our best scholars is that it is not from his pen, although a most valuable contribution to the literature of the New Testament.

So the first big area of concern of these General Epistles, addressed as they are to the continuing Christian church, is to minister to the natural human tendency to take one's faith for granted and either participate less and less in Christianity or slip out of it entirely into nonreligious or even irreligious forms of living.

A second problem arising out of the transfer of Christianity from one generation to another is the loss of freshness and urgency of the original message. Christians of the first generation had a great experience. They were, as we have said, witnesses *of* great things and became witness *to* them *unto* the uttermost. But how much of this freshness and urgency were they able to transmit to their children? The ability to help persons of each new generation discover Christianity for themselves as a new and vital experience is a real problem.

In the Epistle of James one of the great concerns is that Christians actually put their faith to work, make real and genuine the faith they have received and hold it not in word only, but in deed. In illustration after illustration, the author of this practical little epistle tries to get Christians to see their religion working out in the actual affairs of life. This is one way later generation Christians can revive something of the vitality of the original converts.

Another way of getting at this problem is to revive and recapture for the new generation the vital meaning of the theological doctrines of the church. One of these doctrines which quite naturally began to grow dimmer and dimmer with the passage of time was the vivid belief in the early return of Christ. The Epistle of Second Peter tackled this problem in its third chapter. First it recognized that there are those who scoff at the doctrine, asking skeptically why it has not happened yet. The author reminded them that the coming of Christ is geared to God's timetable, not man's, and that with God a thousand years are as a day. In God's eyes, not much time has elapsed. He is working out his eternal purposes regardless of the impatience and cynical remarks of man. The author pointed out that, after all, we should see that the delay of the end of the age, the judgment and all that accompanies it, is really a sign of God's forbearance. He is giving that much more chance for people to come to their senses, learn their lesson, and repent. By reinterpreting for each generation the meaning and present relevance of the great doctrines of the faith, later-generation Christians can keep their Christianity alive and growing.

A third major problem found in these epistles is the presence of many counterfeit forms of Christianity; heresies, we call them. We should clarify our terms. These days we often use heresy either in joking or in a complimentary way, and it is easy to see why we do. So often any kind of creativity which challenges the *status quo* is thought of as a heresy. Actually, a heresy may be the judgment of God upon an established order that has gone stale or empty. Entrenched and institutionalized pride, wealth, and power always brand anyone who challenges them as *heretic* and the history of the church contains the story of a great many true martyrs of the Christian faith who were regarded as heretics in their day.

But what we are talking about here is not this kind of heresy which is really an attempt to recover some valid aspect of Christianity. Rather we shall see the term in its true historical meaning of some distortion of Christianity or substitute for it. In the First Century, among second- and third-generation Christians, this destructive kind of heresy was rife. Even from very earliest times in Paul's day there had been those who wanted to make Christianity into an exacting legalism or flatten it out into a broad permissive relativism. But after Paul's day such tendencies were consolidated into actual movements. One of these, a rather broad school of thought, came to be known as Gnosticism. Basically, Gnosticism was an attempt to combine Christianity with various philosophies and mythologies long current in the Graeco-Roman world — give Christianity a more cosmic character by tearing it loose from the Hebrew moorings and investing it with an elaborate system of beliefs borrowed from the religions of Greece and the Near East. One basic belief of these religions was that matter is evil and spirit good. As a result, the Gnostics tended to take one of two diverse directions in their moral life. Some were ascetics, men who tortured the body for the good of the soul. They were against marriage and sex as evil, and set up elaborate rules of conduct. Still others seemed to have gone in the opposite direction. If the body is of no real significance, they reasoned, why not indulge it freely and have a life of pleasure in this tabernacle of evil?

So attractive were the teachings of Gnostics that many Christians were infected by them even while remaining within the church. Others left the church and joined up with one or another of these movements. A still further threat was the reception of Gnostics into Christianity without their giving up their former mythologies.

We can give only one or two examples of the way in which the General Epistles deal with such a problem. One form of Gnosticism, springing from the belief that the flesh was evil and only the spirit good, was that the Son of God could not have come in flesh, as the gospel has it, but he only *seemed* to. The incarnation was in appearance only, hence the name "docetists," from the Greek word "to seem." Docetists, while attempting to preserve the divine nature of Christ, actually denied his real humanity. Their belief, if allowed to continue, would destroy the historical rootage of Christianity, and would make it a mythological religion. The Gospel of John was written against such a belief. Right from the start it strongly affirmed: "And the Word became flesh and dwelt among us."

The Epistles of John also were written against this kind of heresy. In First John there is a clear-cut description of the docetists whom the author was quite explicit in calling "antichrists," for they denied that Christ had come in the flesh. Second John is concerned about the problem of receiving such false teachers into the church groups, for they were certain to gain entrance and tear the church apart.

The other expression of this Gnosticism, as we have already seen, ran to immorality and looseness. The Epistle of Jude was written to combat heresy of this sort. This little epistle is a masterpiece of well-chosen invective and colorful epithet. After calling these perverters of Christianity licentious, arrogant, and quarrelsome, with a poetic flourish the author called them "fruitless trees in late autumn, twice dead, uprooted; wild waves of the sea, casting up the foam of their own shame; wandering stars for whom the nether gloom of darkness has been reserved for ever." The trouble with a genuine heresy is that it counterfeits the real thing and can deceive even good, sincere Christians.

The danger that threatens later-generation Christianity is the perversion of the true faith by inroads from within and without which may make a sort of hodgepodge of it and in the end pervert it out of all recognition. It was Jude who coined the phrase "the faith which was once for all delivered to the saints" as expressive of mainstream Christianity which is to be preserved if the authentic Christian witness is to persist upon the earth.

Still a fourth major problem which threatens Christianity as it passes from one generation to another is pressure from without to discourage the faithful from their faith. We might use the general term "persecution" to describe this problem, especially as we see it ranging all the way from mere social pressure and discrimination to actual violence and death.

One of the epistles which tells of a persecution that was still in its less violent stages, but which might get hot later is First Peter. Whether the epistle refers to the days of Nero or to one of the later times of tension between the church and the pagan society about it, we cannot be absolutely sure. What we do know is that the Christians depicted here were under various forms of social and psychological pressures by their pagan neighbors. One of the weapons used was ridicule. Those who abandoned their former ways of living and became Christians were taunted by their old associates. "They are surprised that you do not now join them in the same wild profligacy, and they abuse you" (1 Peter 4:4). Another type of pressure is just plain misunderstanding, ignorant criticism of Christians. Some of the wildest stories got around because Christians in the pagan world behaved differently from their neighbors. Kindness was easily interpreted as weakness, genuine concern for the helpless and needy was taken as sentimentality or worse. Partly because the pagans just could not understand what the transforming love of God had done for these Christians and partly out of guilty conscience which had to vent itself in spiteful acts against them, they discriminated against Christians, criticized and attacked them. The concern in First Peter is that by Christlike spirit and good conduct the Christians shut the mouths of their critics and prove what is right in the crucible of everyday living (1 Peter 2:15; 3:16).

As we well know, persecution did not stop with mere social and psychological pressures. Often persecution became the shedding of blood. This life-and-death struggle of Christianity is also mentioned in these latter books of the New Testament. In First Peter we read of the "fiery trials" coming upon the Christians. Hebrews speaks of former days of persecution and suffering, calls the roll of the faithful who have endured through untold hardships, and then urges readers to be ready for whatever tests and trials lie ahead (Heb. 10:32-12:11). It is not, however, until we come to the Book of Revelation, the last one printed in our New Testament, that we find the issue of persecution unto death and the terrific struggle of Christians fully spelled out. In fact, this book, so highly dramatic and symbolic, seems to gather up most of these features of later-generation Christianity. Written to prepare Christians toward the end of the first century to face courageously a titanic struggle between the church and the Roman Empire, the writer introduced his message in the form of letters from the risen Lord to the seven churches of Asia. In these letters he urged Christians to appreciate and value their faith (our first point in this chapter), to rekindle their first love (our second point), and to get rid of all heresy (our third point). All this was a preparation for enduring the hardships that would soon be coming upon them as the clash with Rome developed. In this book witnesses become *martyrs* as they persist in witnessing to the uttermost.

For many Christians today, Revelation is a closed, mysterious, or even forbidding book. Others have found it too fascinating and can think or speak of little else, taking it, unfortunately, as an exact blueprint for present-day events. What it really was intended to be was a tract for its own times to prepare Christians to live through a tremendous crisis without hysteria or backsliding. Thus understood, it can serve as an inspiration for us today in the period of crisis in which we live and may continue to live for some time. Once we are acquainted with and accept its literary artform (the apocalyptic, a highly impressionistic and symbolic form), its message comes through loud and clear. Here is evil in all its horrendous forms. Here are political and military power in all their demonic expression. But there also are the forces of good: the transcendent and all-wise God, his Son Jesus Christ, and Christ's body, the church. And God, through Christ and the church, will triumph over all enemies, said the Revelator. The Lamb, slain from the foundation of the world, is on the throne victorious (Rev. 5:6; 22:5) and he shall reign for ever and ever, hallelujah! This triumph is no escape from suffering and crisis, but a resolute facing of calamity and destruction with triumphant faith, a finding in the sovereign God the theme for a mighty hallelujah chorus for all heaven and earth.

In summary, we have seen the church of the subsequent generations already reflected in the New Testament. It faced several problems peculiar to second- and third-generation Christians: (1) a tendency to take Christianity for granted, (2) a loss of original urgency and freshness, (3) a possibility of a counterfeit or mixed Christianity and (4) the danger of backsliding or growing hysterical under various degrees of persecution.

The early church soon became the church of succeeding generations, the church of all the centuries down to and embracing our own day. Its story is our story. Its source of power in God, Christ, and Holy Spirit is our source and its problems are our problems as we today also face the future.

APPENDIX

1. The Community of the Resurrection

Suggestions for Study:

Acts, Chapter 1.

Albert, C. Winn, *Acts of the Apostles,* (Layman's Bible Commentary, Vol. 20), John Knox Press, pp. 16-28.

William Barclay, *The Acts of the Apostles,* (The Daily Study Bible Series), The Westminster Press, pp. iii-xix, and 1-12.

The Interpreter's Bible, Vol. 9, Exegesis of The Acts of the Apostles by G. H. C. Macgregor, pp. 23-35.

F. J. Foakes-Jackson, *The Acts of the Apostles,* Harper and Row, pp. 1-10.

W. C. van Unnik, *The New Testament,* Harper and Row, pp. 117-148.

For further thought and discussion:

What more is there, if anything, to the resurrection of Christ than just a victorious idea?

What would it mean for your church group today to be truly a community of the resurrection?

Where are we as individuals and as groups on this matter of being witnesses-of, witnesses-to, and witnesses-unto-the-uttermost in our relation to the gospel of Christ?

2. The Church and Fearless Witness

Suggestions for study:

Acts 2 — 5.

Winn, *Acts of the Apostles,* pp. 28-55.

Appropriate sections of Barclay, Foakes-Jackson, and the *Interpreter's Bible.*

Howard C. Kee and Franklin W. Young, *Understanding the New Testament,* Prentice-Hall, Inc., pp. 184-189, 192f.

Morton Enslin, *Christian Beginnings,* Harper & Row, pp. 175-177

For further thought and discussion:

How is the Holy Spirit poured out on people today?

What will it take to make us forthright, fearless Christians like those of the first century?

How can our witness today be fearless and effective without being narrow and bigoted?

3. The Church and Economic Problems

Suggestions for study:

Acts 2:43-47; 4:32 — 5:11; 6:1-7.

Winn, Barclay, Foakes-Jackson, and MacGregor *(Interpreter's Bible)* on these passages.

Kee and Young, pp. 189-192.

For further thought and discussion:

What permanent contribution, if any, do you see in the Jerusalem community of goods?

Are economic issues in society outside the church the legitimate concern of the church today? If not, where do our responsibilities to people end? If so, what can and should the church do about them?

4. The Church Breaks With Provincialism

Suggestions for study:

Acts 6:8 — 8:40.

Winn, Barclay, Foakes-Jackson, and Macgregor on this portion of Acts.

On *Samaritans* in particular:
John 4:9; 8:48; Luke 9:51-55; 10:33-37; 17:11-19.
Kee and Young, pp. 196f.

For further thought and discussion:

With what groups today do you or anyone of your

friends sustain a "Samaritan" relationship? What does the gospel prompt you to do about it?

What is the connection between provincialism and egotism? Where does thinking of persons with labels attached to them fit into this scheme?

How are provincialism and prejudice to be overcome without erasing some very real and valuable human particularities?

5. The Church and the Gentile Challenge

Suggestions for study:

Acts 9 — 12.

Winn, Barclay, Macgregor, and Foakes-Jackson on the key passages of Acts 10 and 11.

Kee and Young, pp. 199-203.

For further thought and discussion:

What "Gentile" lines of demarcation do we as Christians face today?

How are religious lines to be crossed or overcome without blurring valid moral and spiritual distinctions?

How does God lead men today in transcending religious and cultural lines of separateness?

6. The Church Faces the Complex Roman World

Suggestions for study:

Acts 13 — 14.

Discussion of pertinent passages in these chapters by Winn, Barclay, Foakes-Jackson, and Macgregor.

Kee and Young, pp. 221-230.

Wm. R. Halliday, *The Pagan Background of Early Christianity,* Cooper Square Publishers, Inc., pp. 30-63.

C. K. Barrett, ed., *The New Testament Background, Selected Documents,* Harper-Row, pp. 1-21, 29-35.

For further thought and discussion:

What aspects of Roman civilization remind you of American society?

In those aspects in which American culture resembles the ancient Roman, what serious problems does the gospel encounter as it attempts to penetrate our society?

How are we to correct any distortions of the gospel which have resulted from the treatment modern American society has given it?

7. The Church and Unity Through Diversity

Suggestions for study:

Acts 15.

Winn, Barclay, Foakes-Jackson, and Macgregor on this chapter.

Kee and Young, pp. 236-239.

For further thought and discussion:

When sincere Christians differ, how are they to find the will of God, and be sure they have found it?

How should any group of Christians go about securing the proper balance between *freedom* (to differ, to be themselves) and *order* (unity and structure)?

How does the true ordering of the life of the church differ from purely secular democratic processes?

8. The Church and the Greeks

Suggestions for study:

Acts 16 — 17.

Winn, Barclay, Foakes-Jackson, and Macgregor on these chapters.

Kee and Young, pp. 240-256.

For further thought and discussion:

What similarities do you find between the ancient Greek mind and that of Americans today? What differences?

How can the church today combat superstitions on the one hand and skepticism on the other?

In what ways does true Christianity stand over against

"the American mind" today in both judgment and transformation?

9. The Church and the Big City

Suggestions for study:

Acts 19:1-41; 20:17-28.

These chapters in Winn, Barclay, Foakes-Jackson, and Macgregor.

Kee and Young, pp. 257-265.

Interpreter's Bible, Vol. 10, pp. 3-8.

For further thought and discussion:

Which of the problems that Paul encountered in the city are still with us today in our urban church work?

What new problems in urban living do you think have arisen since the days of Paul? What light does the gospel shed on their solution?

If Christianity is not to lose out in our inner city areas, what must happen?

10. The Younger and the Older Churches

Suggestions for study:

Acts 19:21f; 20:1-6.

1 Corinthians 16:1-4; 2 Corinthians 8 — 9; Romans 15:25-27.

Winn, Barclay, and Foakes-Jackson on the passages in Acts.

Other commentaries on 2 Corinthians 8 — 9.

Kee and Young, pp. 265-267.

For further thought and discussion:

What are the responsibilities of any newly formed Christian fellowship (at home or overseas) to the older churches which gave it birth?

What should be the relation between the "sending" churches and the "receiving" churches in the worldwide mission program of the church today?

How may Christians around the world, from both the older and younger churches, really get along together without being either provincial or patronizing toward one another? How may we deal with this problem?

11. The Church as a Legal Revolution

Suggestions for study:

Acts 21 — 26.

Winn, Barclay, Foakes-Jackson, and Macgregor on key incidents in these chapters.

Kee and Young, pp. 300-317.

For further thought and discussion:

To what extent is Christianity today both legal and revolutionary?

How may our American Christianity preserve the cutting edge of the gospel and still not be subversive of the best in American society?

How is the church going to bring about a true revolution in our day so as to prevent a nuclear war and race suicide?

12. The Church and Rome

Suggestions for study:

Acts 27 — 28.

Commentary on these chapters, particularly on 28:11-31, in Winn, Barclay, Foakes-Jackson, and Macgregor.

Kee and Young, pp. 300-317.

For further thought and discussion:

What happens to Christianity when it becomes respectable and accepted in centers of power and authority?

How is Christianity to remain true to Christ when it gains power and prestige?

What should be the Protestant attitude toward Roman Christianity today?

13. The Church and Succeeding Generations

Suggestions for study:

Hebrews, James, 1 and 2 Peter, 1 John, Jude, Revelation.

Commentaries, and books you may have introducing these epistles.

Kee and Young, pp. 325-352.

Enslin, pp. 308-311; 321-323; 335f; 339-342.

For further thought and discussion:

Which of the problems of the first-century church, as it crossed the generations, is still with us today?

How is the Christianity of a later generation to preserve the freshness and power of the original church?

What kind of revival does our Christianity of the twentieth century need? When and how is it going to get it?